Book
builder

Book builder

The definitive guide to writing the book to transform your business

Lucy McCarraher and **Joe Gregory**

Foreword by Daniel Priestley

R^ethink

First published in Great Britain in 2020
by Rethink Press (www.rethinkpress.com)

Contents

Foreword

The book that changes your life the most is not one that you read, it's one that you write. No amount of consuming articles, blogs, podcasts or books will come close to the impact of what you produce. Writing and publishing a book is a powerful step in your career or business.

In 2010, my first book *Become a Key Person of Influence* was published and since that time I've had countless opportunities come from it. It's helped me to meet amazing people, get featured in the media, speak on big stages and scale a business globally.

I've also seen first-hand what a vital tool a published book is for many other business owners. Being the author of a good book is one of the best ways I've found to effortlessly demonstrate your value, attract more interest, increase your influence and raise your income. In fact, that first book had such a huge impact on my business that I've since written or co-authored five more, the next two of which were snapped up and published by Wiley. More recently, I've published a further three books with Rethink Press; hybrid publishing proved itself to be the better option.

A book is a powerful asset for attracting clients. I liken my books to a first meeting over coffee with people. My books go out into the world and network with people, share key ideas and in many cases provide a direct sales enquiry to our team. An essential part of our marketing strategy is to send out hundreds of books each month to people that I wish I could meet personally.

A book is brilliant for attracting great people onto your team or helping to train new recruits. Sir Richard Branson agrees. He said that his recent business book *The Virgin Way* was written as a culture-building tool for the 60,000 people who work at Virgin more than the general public. Many of these 60,000 people first fell in love with the brand when they read a book like *Screw It, Let's Do It* or *Losing My Virginity*.[1]

---

1   Richard Branson, *The Virgin Way: How to listen, learn, laugh, and lead* (Random House, 2014); *Screw it, Let's Do It: Lessons in life* (Virgin Books, 2006); *Losing My Virginity* (Virgin Digital, 2011)

A book creates credibility and authority. It tells the world that the creator is an authority in their field. It's no coincidence that the word 'authority' has the word 'author' in it. Having worked with thousands of entrepreneurs, professionals and leaders across fifty industries, in over a dozen countries, we've found that over a third of our clients who publish a book double their income in under two years.

The process of writing makes you smarter: it sharpens communication skills, develops a thought-leadership stance and clarifies thinking around themes and trends on a topic.

In a study of forty leaders Dent has worked with, all of those who wrote books claimed they gained significantly more credibility in their field as a result. This translated into tangible benefits like paid speaking engagements, media attention and increased prices.

For all of these reasons you are making a wise decision to write a book and you've also come to the right place for support in doing it well.

Lucy McCarraher has been the Publish Mentor for Dent and the Key Person of Influence programme since 2013. She and Joe Gregory have mentored hundreds of entrepreneurs through their inspired system of planning and writing business books and published them through Rethink Press. I work with Lucy and

Joe to produce and publish my books: they take my rough draft manuscript and turn it into a high-quality publication. With decades of experience, they know all the tweaks and refinements that go into creating a successful book. In the UK business book charts, at any given time you'll see a number of their titles in the top ten best sellers because they know what works.

When you work with successful, experienced suppliers of award-winning products to build your assets, life gets easier. You don't have to learn or pretend to be an expert in publishing yourself or tie up your intellectual property and royalties with old school publishers when you have experts like Joe and Lucy. They know what the industry trends are and how to write and produce books that are valuable assets for the long term.

While the barriers to entry for writing and publishing a book are now lower than ever, the barriers to excellence have never been higher. There are more books competing for your market's attention, people can share their review with the world in an instant, and retailers are continuing to innovate to weed out the good content from the bad.

So, if you intend to write a book you can be proud of to raise your authority and get your message out to your audience in a big way, I urge you to read *Bookbuilder* – the latest and most refined methodology for planning, writing and publishing an excellent business book from the pre-eminent experts in the field.

In a global marketplace powered by digital platforms, published content is the key to attracting highly valuable opportunities from far and wide, and a book is the supreme published format. There's no doubt, if you are embarking on the journey of writing your book, you can look forward to many rewards.

Daniel Priestley, bestselling author, entrepreneur and founder of Dent Global

Introduction

Nothing sells you like a book.

Working with hundreds of entrepreneur authors, we have seen again and again the power of books to inspire, inform and transform lives and business, and we want to encourage and enable more of you to do this easily and well.

We've watched small – and not so small – businesses flourish and grow and become smarter, more agile, increasingly professional and successful. We've seen their owners gain confidence and become more creative, savvy and mature in regard to their business practice. And we know one of the reasons for this is that increasing numbers of coaches, consultants, entrepreneurs and experts share their insights and expertise through writing and publishing books on their specialist subjects. They are generous with their information: they spread the word about good practice, smart processes, innovative leadership and management, and insightful self-development. Writing your book and sharing your knowledge spreads value through the business community and beyond to your varied markets and clients.

We are the Founders of Rethink Press, the premier hybrid publisher of business books in the UK and with a growing international presence. To be clear, when we talk about 'business books' we mean books written by experts that grow their impact, income and influence, and transform their businesses – they can be on any subject, business or otherwise.

We both started ground-breaking publishing companies early in our careers.

Lucy was at university when she co-founded Australia's first national theatre magazine that was published monthly for eight years straight, a feat that no one has repeated since. After she returned to the UK, she worked for Methuen, literary agency Cruickshank Cazenove, in and on TV and video, and had her first two books published when she was a work-life-balance expert. She has since published three novels, two more self-help books, and six books on writing and publishing, including *A Book of One's Own* to encourage more women writers.[2] She is the Publish Mentor for Dent Global's Key Person of Influence programme, and in 2017 she founded the Business Book Awards to celebrate the achievements of authors and the publishing industry in this important sector.

Joe, a designer and copywriter, had been running a successful digital agency since 1997. He turned to publishing full-time in 2003 when he sold thousands of copies of his first self-published book on marketing. Bookshaker took a cutting-edge approach to publishing, signing up not well-known or broad-market authors but coaches, consultants and entrepreneurs with niche audiences and goals for their books beyond retail sales. Joe saw how the new print-on-demand technology and online retail platforms could disrupt the established model of publishers and bookstores as gatekeepers and open the market to a new range of authors. His most recent book, *Make Your Book Pay*,[3] is the definitive guide to using your book to sell you and your business.

In 2011, we joined forces and founded Rethink Press on a hybrid business model: authors would pay for the production of their books, keeping them in control of the design and positioning, owning all copyright

---

2   Lucy McCarraher, *A Book of One's Own: A manifesto for women to share their experience and make a difference* (Rethink Press, 2019)
3   Joe Gregory, *Make Your Book Pay* (Rethink Press, 2021)

in their intellectual property (IP) and with the specific aim of using their books as business tools. In partnership with Dent and the Key Person of Influence programme, we have published over 400 titles and developed a unique full service for entrepreneurs who want to plan, write and publish their transformative business books.

The adage that 'everyone has a book in them' is nonsense. The vast majority of people don't have the content or skills to write a book – or at least one worth reading. And the fact is that for all those people, especially in the business community, who tell you they're going to write a book one day, or even that they're currently writing their book, only a small percentage act on and complete their goal.

There are two reasons for this: the first is that they're not in the right position to produce a good business book – and a bad book can be worse than no book at all. If your business is in start-up mode, and you don't have deep experience, a proven process, a clear client base or your own case studies to support your assertions, you might want to take a couple of years to gain the requisite resources and IP before committing it to book form. Having said that, the occasional unicorn turns an exceptional concept into a book and builds a stunning business on the basis of their published vision.

If your business is already established and successful, your client journey regularly produces positive outcomes, your industry knowledge is substantial, and you are ready to move into a new phase of visibility and achievement, then you have no excuse for not writing and publishing your book – indeed, it could be seen as selfish not to share your valuable insight with the world.

But it may be that what has been stopping you is the second and most common reason that most people either never get started or fail to finish writing their book: simple lack of know-how – how to write the right book, and how to position, plan, build, write and publish a book that will establish your thought leadership and take you and your business to the next level. And this is where we come in. Having mentored hundreds of authors through their book creation and production, we have developed a unique and streamlined process that will guarantee your book's success.

As an entrepreneur, founder, coach or consultant, your book has a number of goals, all of which are congruent with selling your core business but go further: it must make you the authority in your industry; it differentiates you from your competitors; it should bring you visibility, media attention and speaking opportunities; and it should establish you as a provider of knowledge and value *above and beyond* your products and services. The very act of planning and writing your book may also clarify, expand and sometimes even pivot your business.

A book is a product with a price tag that many readers will have actually paid, which means there is a crucial difference between an overt pitch for business and a published book. A book is perceived as an authority piece in a way that no video, blog, podcast, social media, white paper or other medium can match, and it's vital not to devalue that.

What we will show you in *Bookbuilder* is how to make your book your best sales tool ever – but as an undercover operator. We will enable your book to speak directly to your ideal client, but without ignoring other readers. It will be packed with case studies, but never testimonials. It will outline your unique process, but never pitch products or services. It can include links to free extra content, but never upsell. It will insulate against 'objections' because its content is completely convincing but not coercive. A reader outside your ideal client avatar is satisfied by the value of the book and won't feel that the secret sauce is only available at a higher price tag. It won't get one-star reviews on Amazon from readers who feel they've paid for what they see as a marketing brochure.

The book we will teach you how to write will be an original, professional product, full of authentic experience and genuine IP. It might be a picture book; it might be your own inspirational story; it might be your disruptive insight; it might be a dip-in-and-out manual; it might be based on your existing content of blog posts, interviews or podcasts. Most often it will be a walk through your distinctive client process backed up by your unique industry vision. Our tried, tested and proven process, from the 3 Ps of Position all the way to the WRITER process, allows any of these formats to emerge from a range of authors without dictating any of them.

The business books we publish have increased in quality, as well as quantity, over the years. We have helped business authors to become more sophisticated writers who can better engage their readers and take them on an enlightening journey. And these smart books have in turn stoked a real hunger in their readers. In conversations and on social media, businesspeople are always sharing and on the lookout for the latest information and insights their peers and mentors have put into print.

In a virtuous circle, our entrepreneur authors have inspired us to refine our coaching and publishing services to meet their needs and those of the voracious readers that they service. In this book we will show you how to be an exceptional Bookbuilder, crafting your manuscript to the highest standards to produce a book that is a game-changer for you, your brand, your business and your readers.

Nothing sells you like a book. But it has to be a good book. We're going to show you how to build your book the right way.

PART ONE
PLANNING YOUR BOOK

One of the most common reasons would-be authors either never get started or write a 'one-page book' – where they start writing but lose focus and never finish – is that they start without a plan. We want to ensure you're clear on why you should write your book and whether now is the time to become an author. Understanding the key elements that will create a transformational book is essential to a successful outcome, as are positioning your book to your core market and planning its content in great detail. This section is as rigorous as the one on Writing Your Book; as you read it, you will understand why and how important planning is as a first step.

1
Book Benefits

Make no mistake, writing and publishing a great book that will transform your business is an intense project. You will need to invest time, money, mental rigour and emotional resilience over a period of time. But the benefits it will bring you, your business, your clients, colleagues, family and friends are exceptional. We want to run through these with you to make sure you're clear on *why* you should write your book and to ensure these outcomes align with your goals.

The idea of writing your book can be daunting. What if nobody is interested? What if your ideas are judged badly? Who are you to be writing a book? Fear can sometimes keep us safe; but, if you're working with professionals, writing and publishing your book will boost your confidence, credibility and clarity. You might worry that your knowledge and content is not fresh and interesting, but your core market will find it extremely valuable and your professional status will be enhanced by becoming an author.

A lack of time or resources might be holding you back. Perhaps you still haven't prioritised your book highly enough in your business plan. What will it take to make your book the most urgent thing on your to-do list? What could happen if you write your book? The more important question is: What could happen if you *don't* write your book but your competitor does?

Your book is a vital business tool, and every day you put off writing it and getting it published you're losing the opportunity to connect with your target audience. Remember, if you don't write your book, you're missing out on business opportunities, money, profile building, claiming your IP and new clients. Our experience of publishing the books of hundreds of entrepreneurs tells us that these are the five predictable outcomes you can expect from writing your book. Do they align with your objectives?

Author benefits

Clarity and confidence

Every author we work with finds that the process of planning and writing their books is both personally and professionally illuminating. Organising your thoughts, knowledge, experience and expertise into a detailed configuration – the blueprint of a logical and enlightening journey for your reader – can be a hard exercise, but it is always rewarding. It forces you to interrogate the steps of your process, your client or customer journey, and the way you want to present your practice and your data to your readers. Is this something you want to achieve?

Writing the manuscript through several iterations then gives you the opportunity to unpack and review everything, from the currency of your views to the whole premise of your business. The book-writing process has triggered a considerable number of entre- preneur authors into re-positioning or pivoting their businesses – for the better and often the bigger. This could be a daunting thought, but you shouldn't be afraid of growing and improving your business.

Having written your manuscript – even if no one else ever reads it – can bring a new level of confidence in a wide range of situations. Your book is probably the most extended piece of writing you will do. It creates an archive of content that you can repurpose into blog posts, articles, podcasts, workshops, courses, presentations and keynote speeches, saving you time and assuring you that whatever format you deploy your edited book manuscript in, it will be the most eloquent and articulate formulation of your knowledge.

What's more, pitching, presenting, speaking and training all become easy, or easier, when you've written your book. Through the writing process – including formulating your thoughts into sharp headings, coherent sentences and flowing paragraphs; illustrating them with appropriate and well-formed case studies and anecdotes; using your own story to underpin your learning journey; and accumulating supporting research and data – you save all this content to the cloud drive in your head and can easily recall and present it in the appropriate situation. A note or a heading on a PowerPoint slide is enough to trigger the section or story you wrote in your book in familiar, easy-to-deliver phrases. A question from the audience or a roomful of decision-makers can be fluently answered with the process you laid out in the book. Even if you are someone who speaks more fluently than you write, you will still have ordered your material more logically and methodically on the page.

Authority and influence

There is nothing that confers the status of authority or expert in your field like being the author of a published book. In this increasingly online environment, your printed book stands out as a physical product, representing you as well as containing your knowledge and skill in a classic and respected medium. Your e-book is an electronic asset that can be given to prospects, clients, colleagues and partners at the touch of a key. And your audiobook speaks your voice of authority directly into the ear of your listeners.

Your book's ability to go far and wide, across continents, speak to people you don't know and would never be able to contact, and be passed on through recommendations and online booksellers to ideal clients, is an extraordinary kind of influence.

Everyone respects an author, even more than we might imagine. In the world of entrepreneurs, it's common to talk about writing a book, and many business owners, coaches and consultants aim to do so. They may take the first steps, pay to go on courses, or get coaching to write their book – but those who actually finish writing their books and get them published are still a small, elite minority, which makes us all the more valued and authoritative.

CASE STUDY – INFLUENCING THE INFLUENCERS

Adam Hamadache, a consultant in the hotel industry, wrote *Give Your Guest A WOW!* and his ideas on customer service were so far-sighted and widely applicable that his book has sold consistently well within and outside of his niche market.[4] It has brought him business, raised his profile, and made him a respected influencer in his industry. Because of his book, Adam is regularly flown to give £1,000+ speaking gigs at top hotel industry events at home and abroad, where he gets to tell established influencers how to up their customer service game. And they take his advice – because he is the author of an excellent and professional book.

Prospects and clients

The well-leveraged book is the best business card and marketing brochure combined, and it pre-sells you and your services to your ideal clients.

By demonstrating your in-depth knowledge and effective process or working model through an engaging reader journey, with plenty of practical case studies, personal anecdotes, and data or research to back up your own experience, the clients you most want to work with – the ones who can most benefit from your

---

4   Adam Hamadache, *Give Your Guest A WOW!* (Rethink Press, 2013)

services and will be willing and able to pay your top rates – will be compelled to contact you.

Your book also acts as a recruitment tool, telling prospective partners, service providers and colleagues what your values and vision are, how your business operates, how you work with clients and what will be expected of them if they want to be a part of your world.

Speaking and platforms

If you would love to get more or better-paid or higher-profile speaking engagements, writing and publishing your book will help you achieve this, too. Every day, we see experts and pundits appearing in the media, and almost inevitably they're introduced as 'the author of...' Their book is the source of their authority to comment on their specialist subject. Not only does their book define their expertise, but it's likely how the programme producer or journalist found them in the first place.

Amazon has one of the most powerful search engines out there. If you have a book published on Amazon and someone searches for your name online, your book title or key words in the description of your book, Amazon's algorithm ensures that you and your book will appear at the top of the search page.

While your area of expertise may or may not be of interest to the mainstream media, your local radio station and newspaper may love to interview you as a local author, and your own industry will definitely be interested in getting you to speak, take part in panel discussions or run workshops, at home and potentially all over the world. But you need to be pro-active in finding the decision-makers and getting your book out to them.

CASE STUDY - RAISE YOUR PROFILE

Monica Or has written three books on her niche in the hospitality industry. Her books cover all aspects of customer service: *Star Quality Hospitality: The Key to a Successful Hospitality Business*; *Star Quality Experience: The Hotelier's Guide to Creating Memorable Guest Journeys*; and *Star Quality Talent: Inspiring Hospitality Careers*.[5] She has consistently leveraged them to raise her profile and become the go-to expert in her field.

'From having my books published I have been invited to speak abroad at conferences, flown business class, and had accommodation and expenses paid for as well as a speaker fee and large book orders. I have been paid to work with partners to run a Thought Leaders workshop, webinar and white paper. Content from my book has been turned into online courses. My status with my industry peers has been elevated and they now take me

---

5   Monica Or, *Star Quality Hospitality: The Key to a Successful Hospitality Business* (Rethink Press, 2014); *Star Quality Experience: The Hotelier's Guide to Creating Memorable Guest Journeys* (Rethink Press, 2016); and *Star Quality Talent: Inspiring Hospitality Careers* (Rethink Press, 2018)

much more seriously. I have been interviewed for trade magazines and spoken at many conferences. It is now a lot easier to connect with people in my industry: many CEOs and Managing Directors are happy to meet with me and I can contact them directly without having to get past their gatekeepers!'

Monica's advice to authors is: 'Once your book is published, don't be shy, shout about it. Share your knowledge far and wide.'

Book magic

Confidence, authority, influence, clients, income and speaking platforms are all transformational outcomes from writing and publishing your book. From our experience of mentoring and publishing hundreds of entrepreneur authors' business books, we know that these are all results you can expect. Of course, you can publish your book and tell no one and do nothing with it, and perhaps the effect will be minimal, but if you follow the suggestions in Joe's book *Make Your Book Pay* and think creatively about how you can use your book to achieve your goals, all of the above outcomes are entirely predictable.

As well as these predictable outcomes, there are always some unpredictable results of publishing an excellent business book – results that sometimes seem almost magical. Some authors have found their book has put them in touch with their heroes; others have been invited onto government committees, unexpectedly doubled their business, become media pundits – the sky's the limit!

Books build business

Entrepreneurs and small business owners gain in three key areas when they write and publish a professional business or self-help book: impact, income and influence.

Impact

When you pitch to a prospect, walk into an interview with a client or turn up to a media interview, giving your book to the other person will double the impact you have on them. When you give a keynote and hand out free copies of your book, run a course in which the book is included as a resource, or simply reach into your bag and give a signed copy to a useful contact at a networking event, you are exponentially increasing your impact – to those people directly and to all the others they talk to.

Income

By far the greatest financial benefit to entrepreneur authors, and where they get the return on their investment, is the high-level clients and contracts their books attract.

CASE STUDY – THE £50,000 READERS

Marianne Page, business systems expert, wrote a first book called *Process To Profit* outlining her approach to systemising businesses for the benefit of owner entrepreneurs.[6] Within six months, she had gained over £50,000 worth of contracts through three people who read her book: a business owner who had picked it up on holiday and got in touch on his return, anxious to work with her; an old friend who heard Marianne had written a book so read it – and realised how much she could help him; and a franchisee who was recommended it and realised Marianne's system was just what he needed. Since then she has written two more books, *Simple, Logical, Repeatable* and *Mission: To Manage*,[7] because each new book elevates her and her business to new levels of success.

Marianne Page is just one of many small business owners whose books have attracted business, whose prospects come 'pre-sold' on their ideas and want to

---

6   Marianne Page, *Process To Profit: Systemise your business to build a high performing team and gain more time, more control and more profit* (Rethink Press, 2013)

7   Marianne Page, *Simple, Logical, Repeatable: Systemise like McDonald's to scale, sell or franchise your growing business* (Rethink Press, 2017); *Mission: To Manage: Because managing people doesn't need to be mission impossible* (Practical Inspiration Publishing, 2020)

pay high fees for implementation of a strategy they already understand and appreciate.

Many small businesses find it hard to make the transition from working with a select group of clients who know and like them to being sought after by a wider following. When an entrepreneur crafts their knowledge and processes into book form, they reach an audience they would never have the time or opportunity to contact personally. Their book becomes their ambassador, working 24/7 to spread their name and expertise. When someone searches their subject, name or business, it appears on one of the world's most powerful search engines: Amazon. Not just anyone gets their name on Amazon – only those who have actually taken the time and effort to write a book.

Influence

There is nothing like having authored a book to cement your credentials as a thought leader and authority in your market. Have you noticed how most media 'experts' are authors, how speakers and guests at events have at least one book to their name, and how leaders in most industries are likely to have put their ideas into book form?

CASE STUDY – RAISE YOUR MEDIA PROFILE *FROM GOOD TO AMAZING*

Michael Serwa, a life coach, wrote *From Good To Amazing: No bullshit tips for the life you always wanted* specifically to raise his profile with the media as well as potential clients.[8] The book has found its way round the world and into the hands of readers who have become fans. Michael and his tips have been featured in popular magazines and newspapers, and he has his own YouTube channel where he interviews other high-profile coaches in his exclusive Mayfair apartment. 'It's all about the book,' in his opinion.

Becoming a bestselling author and making your fortune

No matter how brilliant your book concept, no matter how many people will benefit from reading your message and how many high-paying clients you will attract through your book, you are unlikely to create a substantial income stream from retail sales of your book. Even our bestselling authors, of which there are a few, don't make money from author royalties that comes close to matching what their book brings them from new clients or other sources. None of them would be able (or would want) to give up their day job and live on the proceeds of their book sales

---

8 Michael Serwa, *From Good To Amazing: No bullshit tips for the life you always wanted* (Rethink Press, 2013)

alone. Even the best-known business book authors – think of Tony Robbins or Brenée Brown – who do sell a lot of books, use them to attract clients to their much more profitable training, coaching and speaking businesses.

Writing a business or self-help book will bring you satisfaction, self-development, respect, business and added value in all manner of ways, but if it's all about the royalty money for you, this may not be the right project.

Summary

The right business book will bring you:

- Clarity and confidence

- Prospects and clients

- Speaking and platforms

- Book magic

- Impact, income and influence

- Sales income – not so much

2
Becoming An Author

The first step in your journey to writing your business book is to be clear on the outcomes you want from this project, in which you are going to invest both time and money. This involves understanding whether you and your business are in the right place to achieve these outcomes at this time, so we're going to start by asking a series of questions that will help clarify this for you.

By the time you have worked through this chapter, you should know whether this is the right time for you to become an author and understand a key framework for creating your game-changing business book.

The right time to write

What should you have in place as a founder, entrepreneur or business owner before you embark on writing and publishing your business book? Running through the following checklists will help you decide.

Your business

1. Do you have experience in business that would be helpful to other people?

2. Have you been operating your business for two years or longer?

3. Do you have a well-defined product or service?

4. Has your business been making a good annual profit for at least two years?

If the answer to three or more of these is no, it might not be the right time to write your book. Taking a little more time to work on your business, getting more experience with clients, and defining your products and services more clearly will give you a better basis for the content of your book. While you're doing this, build your business profile and client base too.

If you've answered no to two or more of these questions, you're nearly ready to write your book, and taking the first step of defining your market (your ideal client) and outlining a structure for your book will help you refine your business processes and better define your products and services. Stick with us.

If the answer to three or all of these questions is yes, your business is in great shape. You know your market, have clearly defined products and services, and have a proven process. Now would be an excellent time to write your book, serve your ideal clients and accelerate your business growth. You can use your book to raise your authority, generate more leads and boost your profile.

Your intellectual property

Your IP is part of your authority and will be the source of the content for your book. Your book will consolidate your IP and, when published, provide indisputable proof that you own the ideas and created them first. Having your content and ideas published is the best way of protecting your valuable IP.

Don't worry about over-sharing and giving your prospects so much information that they won't need to buy your services, or your competitors the ability to steal your IP. The aim of your book is to give your prospects maximum information for them to see that they need to come to you for implementation – something the book can't offer. And making your IP or process public will mean anyone can see that it's yours and you can call out copyright theft.

- Have you built up a wealth of knowledge that offers people value?

- Have you been working in your specialist area for three years or more?

- Do you have a proven process, with clearly designated steps, that you work through with most clients?

- Do people ask where they can find out more about your work or regularly tell you that you should write a book?

If you've answered no to three or more of these questions, your IP may not yet be clear or established enough to form the basis of an authoritative book. You may need to spend more time developing your expertise and in-depth knowledge before writing the book or creating an original piece of IP.

If you can't be sure of two or more of the above, you still have valuable IP, and unpacking it through planning and writing your book could be an ideal way to mature, refine and protect it. Consider working with a Rethink coach to further clarify your processes, systems and procedures, creating models, tools and systems you can own.

With three or more 'yes' answers to these questions, you have well-defined, significant and original content based on your proven process. You are considered an expert in your field and clients seek you out. Now is the time to demonstrate your expertise more widely and protect what is yours by consolidating your IP through writing your business book.

Your content

Do you have enough original and high-value content to form the basis of a successful business book? Ask yourself:

- Do you blog, write articles, or create videos, podcasts or other content?

- Do you have case studies of clients or customers to illustrate your successful outcomes?

- Do you use your own story to inspire others and promote your business?

If none of the above apply to you, it would be a good idea to start building your published content showing who you are, what you know and how you work, while you are working on your book. Create an archive of useful, interesting, unique content that serves your target audience and can be repurposed between the book and other media. The content you write now will form the basis for your book.

If you answered yes to two of the questions above, you are already creating useful content, and getting your book project started will help you to spread your ideas more widely. Consider adding other media to your content creation strategy – repurpose, reuse and recycle. Your first step might be to publish a 'mini book' (8,000 to 12,000 words).

If you can say yes to all of the above, you have the content to write your book. You may not even realise that you are already sitting on a mountain of valuable content. Go through our process to structure your content into a clear book format and you'll find the writing will be easy.

Writing your book

- Do you consider writing one of your top skills and something you enjoy?

- Do you have a great idea for a book and plenty of time to plan and write it?

- Do you have a clear structure for your book and a plan for getting it written?

If your answer's no to all of the above, don't worry. Plenty of people feel they don't have the skills or know-how to write their book alone. That's why you're here and reading our book. If, when you get to the end, you still feel you need support in any or all of the areas we discuss, get in touch and we can help.

It's worth saying that many high-profile authors do not write their own books – for many reasons. They might not have the time as they're running a success-ful, growing business. English might not be their first language, or they might have dyslexia or other barri-ers to the physical writing of their great content.

CASE STUDY – OVERCOMING OBSTACLES TO TELL YOUR STORY

Mark Escott is the founder and CEO of a highly successful organisation that provides therapeutic education and training for young people and families who have experienced trauma. He works in that area because of his own lived experiences of trauma during his own childhood. What he didn't know until later was that one reason he found school so difficult was his undiagnosed dyslexia. With this background, Mark never entertained the idea of writing a book, but he found himself on one of our book-planning workshops and very quickly decided that somehow, he had to do it. He worked with one of our coaches to plan his book in detail and then used our BookSmith* service to get the book written. This meant Mark could speak his book through a series of recorded and transcribed interviews, and the writing of his own content was outsourced to a professional. Mark's book that tells his story as well as outlining the work he does with his ideal clients has helped to build his business and make him a high-profile influencer in his area. He is so proud of having overcome his difficulties to write his book that the story of creating his book has become a moving and popular subject in his speaking gigs.

*Any author who uses our coaching or BookSmith writing service does so in complete confidentiality. Mark gave his permission for us to tell his story.

With one or two of the above questions ticked off, you're in a great place to start work. We'll do our best to fill in the information gaps here or offer further support later.

Yes to all three? Perfect – let's go.

The AUTHOR framework

When we coach individual authors or mentor groups through writing their business or self-help books, we start with our AUTHOR framework to help new and experienced authors focus on the vital aspects of every good business book. By working through the AUTHOR elements, you will be able to start gathering all the right content before we take you through the specific steps to build your book.

You can apply this framework to the book as a whole, and to every element within it, such as a part, a chapter, a subsection, even a case study or an anecdote. The AUTHOR framework holds you to a gold standard of content and function for the book that will transform your business.

AUTHOR stands for: Attention, Understanding, Trust, Help, Order and Reaction. You can use these six points as intentions, features and a checklist to make sure your manuscript overall, and each aspect of it, is achieving what is required to bring value and engagement to your reader.

Attention

How are you going to attract attention to your book from your market, your readers and your industry? Is your book concept and its working title and subtitle going to grab the attention of your ideal clients and other readers; will it stand out in and speak to your market or industry? As you write your book, bear in mind the need to maintain your reader's attention through each section; the content must be relevant to their central question and the way you express it must hold their interest. We'll be looking at this from the title, subtitle and Introduction onwards, where our primary goal is to grab the reader's attention and then never let it go.

Understanding

As we've discussed, to write a successful business book you must have deep knowledge of and empathy with the problems that your market faces and the central questions that your ideal clients are asking and need answered. If you can provide the solutions and answers in your book, you have a captive audience, so conveying your experience and expertise to the reader by showing an understanding of their problems and the big promise they are expecting from you is essential. As you write your book, stay conscious that the beam of your understanding will light the reader's path through your book.

Trust

Your readers must believe that as the expert author you have the authority and credibility to offer solutions that they can trust. Your personal/professional story is a vital element in creating this trust, as are your credentials, qualifications, experience and case studies – the ultimate proof of you having delivered answers and solutions already. We will show you how to incorporate and showcase your trustworthiness while writing your business book. Your readers not only need to trust you and what you're saying, they may also need to learn to trust their own ability to achieve the objectives you're guiding them towards in your book. Stories, case studies and anecdotes of other people like them achieving the results your book promises help build a reader's trust in themselves.

Help

This is the key thing you offer to your ideal clients – your ability to help them move from the difficulty they are currently experiencing to growth and development. Every piece of content in your book must in some way help your readers solve their problems and answer their questions. Your book is their help, and its clear structure, well-developed content, and logical and tested process is how they will get this from you. As you write or edit your first draft, you may find yourself wondering whether some of what you are saying is useful, interesting or relevant to your ideal client. All you have to ask yourself is whether it is helping your reader to answer their question or solve their problem. If the answer is yes, keep going. If you find the answer is no for any part of the book, stop and go back to the last place where the answer was yes.

Order

Your book, and each chapter in your book, needs to have a consistent structure and rhythm to ensure you give your reader what you've promised and make the reading experience as engaging and easy as possible. For now, you just need to know that getting the order right (both in terms of ordering the chapters themselves and placing the content within each chapter in the best order) is critical to producing a well-built book. We will spend a significant amount of time creating a watertight and methodical structure for your book through our BUILD process.

Reaction

When you are planning your book, writing your book, building pre-publication buzz for your book, and when you are getting your book published, selling your published book, getting feedback from readers and wanting them to take action as a result of your book, you are looking for a strong reaction. Following the steps in this book will ensure that you get the reaction you want throughout the process of writing your own business book. From reviewing your first draft to editing your final manuscript, bear in mind the whole time what sort of reaction each aspect of your book might get from your readers – and whether it's the one you want them to have.

Summary

You should write your book when:

- You have a strong business in place
- You have content and IP
- You know you can write your book yourself or with support

The AUTHOR framework will enable you to create a book that:

- Gains **A**ttention from your market
- Displays **U**nderstanding of your ideal clients' problems
- Demonstrates that you are an expert author worthy of **T**rust
- Offers the **H**elp your readers need
- Is **O**rdered in concept and structure
- Gets a **R**eaction from your prospects and industry

3
Position And Title

Now you know what your goals for your book are, and whether you're ready to become an author, the next step in your journey is to determine the right book for you, your business and your market. Perhaps you've always known what your book is going to be about; maybe you wake up with a new idea for a book every morning; or it could be that you've been struggling to come up with what feels like the right idea for any book. In any case, by the end of this chapter you'll know exactly what the right book is for you to write right now. And you will have one or more working title and subtitle ideas to be writing to. We'll look at:

- The 3 Ps of Position

- Creating your book's title and subtitle

The 3 Ps of Position

It takes just three things to get clarity and certainty about what book you should be writing now: we'll show you how to establish who your ideal client is – the *person* you're writing for; what their *pain* – their central question or problem – is; and how to make your book the answer or solution that will satisfy their needs and make them want to come to you for more – your big *promise*. This same information will enable you to come up with a great working title and subtitle.

The intersection between your ideal client and their central question defines your market. The intersection between your ideal client and your big promise is where you've positioned your business. And the way you transform your client's central question into your big promise is your genius.

Once you understand how these elements intersect, you have your book – a book that will appeal to your market, promote your business and be powered by your genius.

Person – your ideal client

The important first step is to clarify exactly who you are writing your book for. Some authors with a broad subject matter can be tempted to say their book is for 'anyone and everyone'. Even a traditional publisher, looking for maximum retail sales, won't be happy with that answer – every book has to be sold from a section or shelf in a bookshop, or a handful of categories on Amazon. But for a business book author, who has other reasons for publishing than to achieve retail sales, it is better to focus on one or two ideal clients as the reader you are addressing.

To position your book to your market, consider:

- Your ideal client's business or type of business

- Their position in your / their industry

- Your ideal client's turnover or income (an amount below which they're unlikely to be able to afford your services)

- What their top three motivations for using your services would be

Try to define your ideal client's age range, gender and circumstances, and then give a name to a current, past or future ideal client. From this information, it can be helpful to create an avatar of your ideal client – the individual you would love to work with if you have a B2C business, or the decision-maker in a business you would most like as a client if you work B2B. They may be a theoretical concept at this point, or they could be someone you know but haven't made contact with yet, or someone who has already been your client and who's the type of client you'd like to attract more of. Write a description, draw a picture or find an actual photo of this client, then keep it in your line of vision as you write your book as a one-to-one conversation with that person. It will also help you find your author voice when you start writing.

Niching your book to a single person won't restrict your audience – it will just direct your valuable information to the people most valuable to you.

Pain – your ideal client's central question

The second part of positioning your book is to establish the central question or problem that your ideal client avatar has. Ask yourself:

- What are your ideal client's biggest problems and what issues they are facing in their business or work?

- How do these problems impact them personally?

- What will happen if their problem persists?

Write down the top three reasons your clients come to work with you, and/or the three most frequent questions your prospects and clients ask you.

Knowing and appealing to your ideal client's underlying problems tells you the position they will be in when they're going to come looking for help through your book; the point in their business or personal journey at which you need to meet them with your solution. This is their central question.

Promise – your big promise to your reader

Thirdly, ask yourself, what is your promise to your reader when they've read your book? What is the underlying solution that all your ideal clients will want you to provide?

To identify that, you need to unpack exactly how you improve their business, work or life. What is the unique solution that you offer your clients; how does it differ from other solutions or challenge conventional wisdom in your area? Write down the three top solutions or interventions you provide to the majority of your clients. List the benefits your readers or ideal clients will get if they take your advice or implement your solution.

This is your big promise, and the subject matter of the book you should be writing right now.

Your book should be aimed squarely at the readership of your ideal client, address the subject of their central question and provide the answer or solution throughout the book with your big promise.

Creating your book's title and subtitle

These three crucial axes determine not only the subject of the book you need to write now; they are also your guide to creating a compelling title and subtitle for your book that will tell your market that your book is for them, and they need to read it now.

Here are three examples of effective titles and subtitles:

From Learner to Earner: A recruitment insider's guide for students wanting to achieve graduate job success by Sophie Milliken[9]

---

9   S Milliken, *From Learner to Earner: A recruitment insider's guide for students wanting to achieve graduate job success* (Rethink Press, 2019)

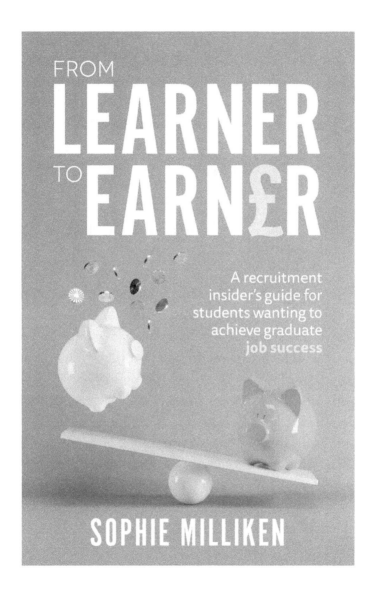

FROM
LEARNER
TO EARN£R

A recruitment
insider's guide for
students wanting to
achieve graduate
job success

SOPHIE MILLIKEN

Sophie's ideal client is a graduate student, demonstrated in the words 'students' and 'graduate'. Their central question is 'How do I get a good job after university or college?' And Sophie's big promise is contained in the dynamic main title, the journey from being a learner to an earner, and in the subtitle wording 'achieve graduate job success'. She also includes her own credentials as the author in the phrase 'a recruitment insider's guide'.

IMPACT: How to be more confident, increase your influence and know what to say under pressure by Dominic Colenso[10]

Dominic's ideal client is clearly someone who either is or wants to be an expert communicator and speaker. Their central question is around how they can increase their confidence when communicating with others and using their platforms to become more influential. Dominic's big promise is superbly condensed in the single word 'impact' – everything his ideal client wants to have. His big promise then speaks to the characteristics his readers desire to feel and embody: confidence, influence, and the ability to find the right words despite the stressful situations they may find themselves in.

---

10 D Colenso, IMPACT: *How to be more confident, increase your influence and know what to say under pressure* (Rethink Press, 2019)

DOMINIC COLENSO

IMPACT

How to be more **confident**, increase your **influence** and know what to say **under pressure**

FOREWORD BY
DANIEL PRIESTLEY

Pull Back Your Power – the ground-breaking code to unlocking profound confidence and soaring success for aspirational women by Anne Whitehouse PhD[11]

---

11 A Whitehouse, *Pull Back Your Power: The ground-breaking code to unlocking profound confidence and soaring success for aspirational women* (Rethink Press, 2019)

Anne's ideal client is a woman either in business or with ambition to succeed in their career. As a scientist herself, who had experienced sexism in academia, she wanted to include all ambitious women, so she used the word 'aspirational' rather than 'business' or 'professional'. Her market's central question relates to lack of confidence and high stress, leading to loss of wellbeing and less successful career outcomes, and her big promise is in her analytical research – hence the word 'code' and the 'PhD' after her name. Her big promise aims to help women feel safe and truly entitled to shine ('profound confidence'), enabling them to take off and fly high ('soaring success'). 'Pull Back Your Power' relates to Anne's key mind-training exercise in the book and also summarises her big promise to women.

Interestingly, though Anne's book is aimed at her ideal client, she has also received heartfelt thanks from women who have been empowered to leave personal situations of domestic violence or coercive control after reading her book – which makes her very happy and goes to show that even if your book is targeted directly at your ideal client, many others will also find value in it.

Title tips

Key words

Start creating your title and subtitle by quickly and intuitively writing one-sentence summaries of:

1. Your ideal client (Person)

2. Their central question (Pain)

3. Your big promise (Promise)

Look at the words you've chosen and decide which are the most impactful and engaging. Write each word on its own card or post-it note and move them around, adding linking words.

Bear in mind the following eight considerations as you select the key words for your title and subtitle:

1. A good title is like a good headline, so model newspapers and magazines.

2. Your title's number one job is to make people want to open the book.

3. Make your title dramatic and use powerful, active and emotive words.

4. Make a big promise or say something shocking or provocative.

5. Ask a leading question to make prospective readers curious.

6. Pose a conundrum that will engage your audience.

7. If you have a clever, witty or one-word main title then your sub-title must explain your book's big promise.

8. Don't try to be clever if a more obvious title is stronger and more engaging.

Twenty power words

Including any one or a combination of these words can power up the impact of your book title and subtitle:

1. How to	11. Unlock
2. Secrets of	12. Beat
3. Stop	13. Free
4. Start	14. You/Your
5. Discover	15. Ways to
6. Unleash	16. The Key to
7. Change	17. The Secret to
8. Never	18. Master
9. Always	19. Become
10. Overcome	20. Learn to

No numbers

Even if your book is based around your five-step, six-key or four-point model, there is little value in making those numbers part of your main title. Remember that your title/subtitle combination has to contain as many keywords as possible that your ideal clients might use to search for a solution to their problem. No one ever searched for 'the five steps to...' to solve their problem or answer their central question, so don't waste three or four words out of the twelve to twenty words you have available.

Also, never use a number in place of a word in a title just so that it matches a website address or product name. 'For' is not the same as '4' and 'to' is not the same as '2'.

Putting all the pieces together

Spend some time coming up with a few titles and subtitles. Mix and match them. Play around with word order. Make sure you don't repeat any words in the title or subtitle as you want to make maximum use of every key word.

Make sure you are positioning your book as a positive solution and focusing on your big promise more than your ideal client's central question. *Bookbuilder – The definitive guide to writing the book to transform your business* is more engaging (we hope) than *How Not To Write the Wrong Book*, for example. The subtitle speaks with authority about being 'the definitive guide' and goes on to reassure that it will be 'the book to transform' the reader's business.

When you've come up with a few ideas, try to whittle them down to three titles and three subtitles. Mix and match them. Try them out on a few close associates – colleagues and current clients, or even prospects that you have a relationship with, are ideal. Your tribe on social media is not – it's too soon to start going public with your book concept.

The combined title and subtitle should meet all of the following five requirements:

1. Clearly indicates what the book is about

2. Makes a big promise

3. Is easy to spell and pronounce

4. Uses simple, dramatic and/or sensational words

5. Is easy to remember and share

Ideally, it should also have at least two of the following qualities:

1. Poses a question

2. Says something contentious, shocking or risky

3. Creates curiosity

4. Is unique and catchy

5. Would work well as a headline in a newspaper or sales letter

Summary

The book that will work for your business should be based on the 3 Ps of Position elements:

- Your ideal client – *Person*

- Your ideal client's central question – *Pain*

- Your big *Promise*

The title and subtitle of your book should also include these elements, and they should:

- Flag to your ideal client that this book is aimed squarely at them

- Focus on your big promise

- Clearly indicate what the book is about

- Contain only keywords and power words

- Be engaging rather than clever

4
Plan And Build

With a clear concept and an engaging and descriptive title and subtitle, we can move on to defining the market and the content for your business book and building the perfect structure that will give you complete clarity. Your structure is your detailed blueprint, and no writing should be done until it is in place. In this chapter, we're going to introduce you to two more models (we like models, and we'll be telling you why you should too):

- The four steps to PLAN your book that helps you get all the vital pieces in place to grab the attention of your ideal readers and offer them your value proposition. It also enables you to immediately write your book's Introduction.

- The unique format we use to BUILD our authors' books from the ground up in layers of contrasting and complementary content.

The PLAN model

Now you have thought about what will attract and retain the attention of your ideal readers, how you will demonstrate your understanding of their problems and gain their trust, and now that you've created an ideal client avatar and know what help they need from you in your book, it's time to take the first step in externalising your work. You could consider it as a basic floor plan of the book you are building.

The PLAN model consists of four steps: Position, Listen, Ambition and Niche Vision. It follows on from the work we've done in Chapter 3 and allows you to instantly create the Introduction to your book and a document you can use to promote your book pre-publication to anyone who asks for information.

Position

There are two parts to the Position step:

Part One – position your book to your ideal client. It's important to start your Introduction or pitch with a clear description of who you are writing your book for. Your ideal client needs to know that you are speaking to them directly, so the first section needs to allow them to identify themselves as the community, however wide or specific, you will bring value to. You've already created an ideal client avatar from the first P of Position in Chapter 3, so just expand on this.

In the first three paragraphs of the Introduction of this book (from 'Nothing sells you like a book...' to 'varied markets and clients'), we hope you have identified yourself as part of 'the entrepreneur community', a founder of one of the 'small – and not so small – businesses', and identify as one or more of the 'coaches, consultants, entrepreneurs and experts' we refer to.

To start the Introduction of your book, write 150 to 200 words addressed to and describing your ideal clients and the target market for your book.

Part Two – this is about how you want to position yourself, explicitly and in detail, and ensure your readers trust you as the expert in your field and author of your book. To clarify your own position of authority, you might want to make some brief notes on: your position in your industry; your unique experience – including any failures as well as successes; external validation of your expertise, such as credentials or qualifications; and the difference between you and your competitors. Mention individuals or businesses that you have helped – name-drop, if possible –

and summarise the outcomes you achieved for these clients.

Now, write 250 to 300 words introducing yourself as the author to your ideal client/reader of your book. As an example, look at the section of our Introduction that starts with 'We are the Founders...' and ends with '... their transformative business books'. This is where we have introduced ourselves and set out our credentials to establish our trustworthiness as authors. This section in our book may be a little longer than it will be in yours because there are two of us.

Listen

The next step is to demonstrate that you have listened to the ideal client you have just defined; are aware of the problem(s) they are facing and how these provided the motivation for you to write your book. Remind yourself what your ideal client wants to achieve in their business or their life, what challenges and problems are stopping them from reaching their goals, and what will happen if their problem persists. Knowing and appealing to your ideal clients' underlying problems tells them you understand the position they will be in when they pick up your book looking for help – the point in their business or personal journey at which you are ready to meet them with your solution.

Now, write 250 to 350 words about your understanding of your ideal clients' challenges or problems, just as we have between the paragraph in our Introduction that starts, 'The adage that "everyone has a book in them" is nonsense' and the one that ends, '... will guarantee your book's success'.

Ambition

Next, ask yourself: What is your ambition for your reader when they've read your book? What is the underlying and detailed solution that all your ideal clients will want you to provide? To define this for them and for yourself, you need to unpack exactly how you improve their business, work or life. What is the solution that you offer your clients, and how does it differ from other solutions or challenge conventional wisdom in your area? List the benefits your readers or ideal clients will get if they take your advice or implement your solution.

In 250 to 350 words, outline to your ideal reader what you offer them in this book and how it will benefit them and/or their business. Give them a taste of the value they are going to gain and make them anxious to read on and get the benefits of your knowledge and experience.

We start this section of our Introduction with the paragraph that opens, 'As an entrepreneur, founder, coach or consultant...' and it continues through to the words, '... they see as a marketing brochure.'

In these paragraphs, we describe our ambition for our readers – to have a business book that will be 'your best sales tool ever' – the prime objective, we believe, of our ideal clients who want to write their business books. Describe for your readers what you and your book will do for them.

Niche vision

Finally, the content of your book will be based on the niche vision that is your unique service, product or concept. What is the process you take all your clients through? Writing it out for your book is a chance to standardise and develop it into defined steps, and perhaps create a model, such as an acronym like AUTHOR, PLAN or the WRITER process (coming in Part Two); a metaphor, like a toolbox or climbing a mountain; a graphic, like the Urgent/ Important matrix or Bloom's Taxonomy; a combination of actions, like the five Ps of the Key Person of Influence programme; or a number of steps like The Twelve Step Programme. Within an overarching process, you may have tools, tips or techniques that are also your own creations – like our 3 Ps of Position or our 3 Ts (coming up in Chapter 5).

Vital to a good business book, which is not overtly salesy but sells you and your services under the radar, are case studies and examples, preferably from your own clients, to illustrate your theories and 'hard' content. Case studies complement the anecdotes and learning points from your own journey.

If you haven't yet developed a model that describes your client journey simply, memorably and concisely, now is the time to work on that. Then, mention this in the final section of your book's Introduction – your final 250 to 350 words. In the final paragraphs of our Introduction, from the one starting, 'The book we will show you how to write will be…' to the end, we can speak with confidence about 'Our tried, tested and proven process', knowing that we have our original framework and models to lead our readers through.

When you have written a few hundred words on each of the topics in the PLAN model, you will have the first draft of the Introduction of your book, which will double as a 'book pitch' while you're writing, and the basis of a press release when your book is launched.

Book**builder** BOOK STRUCTURE

PART ONE
Beginning or Theory
2-5 CHAPTERS
10,000 words

White card Basics text illustrated consistently with Blue Uniques and Green Inspirations. 'Parts' optional.

PART TWO
Middle/Main/Model
2-5 CHAPTERS
10,000 words

White card Basics text illustrated consistently with Blue Uniques and Green Inspirations. 'Parts' optional.

PART THREE
End/Implementation/Outcomes
2-5 CHAPTERS
10,000 words

White card Basics text illustrated consistently with Blue Uniques and Green Inspirations. 'Parts' optional.

CONCLUSION/SUMMARY
500–1,000 words

Main points of your book
What the reader now knows
What the future holds for them
What they should do next
(contact you, further free info...)

BACK MATTER **1,000 words**

References/Further Reading*
Acknowledgements: thank anyone and everyone
The Author *(300 word bio ending in your website and social media contact details + B&W hi res headshot)*

Optional

TOTAL WORD COUNT: 34,000

MAIN CONTENT

On each White Card: the title of an individual topic, equivalent to an article/blog post *(up to 1000 words)*.

ILLUSTRATIONS

To 'illustrate' your White card basics: on each Blue card a personal story, case study, anecdote, quote from
interview *(250 words)*; on each Green card some research, reference to other works, statistics, graph, chart, table.

BOOK CHAPTERS

Group your Basics, Uniques and Inspirations into 6–12 Chapters; on each Pink Card: the title of each Chapter *(descriptive rather than clever)*.

SECTIONS

Take seven Yellow Cards and name them:
Front Matter, Introduction, Part 1, Part 2, Part 3, Summary and Back Matter.

For planning purposes, sort your Chapters (Pink + White, Blue and Green Cards) into three sections. These section headings do not need to appear in the final book.
Part 2 may have more chapters than Parts 1 and 3.

INTRODUCTION **1,500 words**

Who you are *(brief version of your personal/business story)*
Why you're writing the book
Who it's for
What their problem is
How you will solve it *(briefly)*

FRONT MATTER **1,000 words**

Praise quotes *(approx 6 short paras over 2 pages)**
Copyright/imprint page
Contents Page
Dedication *(short)**
Foreword *(500 words, written by someone else)**

Optional

BUILD your blueprint

Here's a basic book structure that the majority of business books will fit into:

If it looks complicated at first glance, don't worry. We're going to deconstruct it for you so you can create your own book structure in a series of simple steps.

When we coach individual authors or train groups of entrepreneurs, we use our BUILD system – a set of bespoke coloured cards when working in person, or our unique MyBookPlan software that represents the cards. We divide the content of a book into the following colour-coded categories and BUILD the book blueprint from the titles of short sections of text.

There are two possible starting points, depending on how clear you are on the structure that your book will follow. If you already have a clear idea of the structure your book will take, particularly if you have a model or framework that describes your process and will underpin the structure of your book (eg steps will be chapters), it may be best for you to start with the Linear category's chapter headings rather than individual topics, and populate your chapter headings later. If you don't yet have a fixed idea about how your book will take shape, start with the Basics.

Basics

On White Cards write the titles of individual topics that you need to tell your ideal client/reader about in your book. Each one should represent a blog-post-type piece of between 500 to 1,000 words. Write the topic names quickly as they occur to you. Don't stop to think about which order they should come in, how much you need to say about each, or whether you will need to research some topics. Just write. When you have thirty to forty topic headings, you have created the building blocks of your book content. Remember that each of these headings is part of the Help that is the fourth step in the AUTHOR framework.

Uniques

On Blue Cards list original content that will illustrate your white-card topics with short 'stories' of your own practical experience. These are like windows for your reader into your unique process, knowledge, experience and personality. The two most important types of Uniques are: short case studies, little vignettes of your successful interventions with your own clients, to be used as practical illustrations of your more theoretical topics; and personal anecdotes, parts of your own business or personal journey, both successes and failures, ups and downs. Sharing these little stories will engage your ideal client and reader in a different way than your Basic content. They will allow them to see that you and your clients have experienced the same challenges that they are facing now, and that you know how to solve their problems in real-life situations. Uniques can also include excerpts from interviews with clients, colleagues, partners or quotes taken from your own research.

Each Unique card represents up to 250 words of storytelling. Ten to twenty of these cards will give your reader an insight into you personally and your work on the ground. These are your undercover sales agents that draw ideal clients back to work with you. Every ideal client reading your book should be able to identify so strongly with three or four Uniques that they will immediately want to get in touch and ask you to help them in the same way.

Inspiration

On Green Cards name quotes, references, ideas and content from other experts that have inspired you, that have contributed to your own work, model or process, and that would be important to reference or useful to point your reader to. These can include books, articles, quotations, models, statistics, graphs, charts, tables and more. They represent the steps in your book-building that have elevated you to a higher level of thinking. These will also illustrate your white-card topics and give support and substance to your views. Remember that other people's work, whether quotations, references or images, must be attributed and referenced, and in some cases, it needs permission to reproduce. You will need to check all these with your publisher or editor.

It's possible that your book won't reference anyone else's work – everything you present is original and straight from your own imagination and experience. But we feel that showing you've read around your subject and been inspired by others gives you more authority.

Linear

The nature of books is that they are read line by line, page by page and chapter by chapter. This is where you put your Basics, Uniques and Inspiration content into the order we mention in the AUTHOR framework – a structured journey for your reader – by sorting them into sequential chapters.

On Pink Cards write the number and name of each chapter that will contain your content and illustrations. These represent the linear steps on your reader's journey. In the building metaphor, they are the rooms into which your interior is divided to make sense of where you are. Between six and fifteen chapters is ideal: fewer than six makes for long chapters; more than fifteen results in short chapters. If you have your model or process defined, the steps should show up as chapter headings. Either start with chapter headings and populate them, or sort existing white, blue and green cards into chapters.

Definition

In the final step, you may want to sort your chapters into two to four overarching 'parts'. This book is divided into three parts – Part One: Planning Your Book, Part Two: Writing Your Book and Part Three: Publishing Your Book – within each of which are several chapters. This final piece of the structure can be viewed as 'levels' or stories in a building, each of which contain a similar if not exactly the same number of rooms.

On Yellow Cards sort your chapters and their contents into overarching parts – eg Part One (three chapters), Part Two (four chapters), Part Three (three chapters). The parts might represent Beginning, Middle and End; or Theory, Model and Implementation. Also add 'Introduction' and 'Summary' on yellow cards – bookending (literally) sections that every book needs.

In the flexible BUILD system, you could have started from the bottom up with white-card Basics, added blue Uniques and green Inspirations, then sorted them into pink chapters and finally divided the chapters into yellow parts. Or you could have started with chapter headings, populated these with Basic, Unique and Inspiration content, then divided them up into parts. Or you could even have worked from the top down, starting with the overarching parts, breaking them down into chapters and finally populating the chapters with the Basic, Unique and Inspiration content.

Your contents page

Once you have finalised your book structure in the card system, an essential next step is to gather your cards and list every single one of them in a detailed contents page.

This is your book blueprint; it will allow you to keep an overview of your book structure as you write and tackle the writing as a 'writing by numbers' exercise. With every element of your content listed out, your first draft will be about filling in the blanks. From the titles of your 250-word case studies to your 1,000-word basics, writing your first draft will almost entirely consist of just getting your existing knowledge out of your head and onto the page – not necessarily even in chronological order.

Here is a summary list of all the elements you should include in your book:

Front matter – 1,000 words

- Praise quotes (approximately six to twelve short paragraphs over two pages – they must be about the book, not you or your business or services)*

- Copyright / imprint page

- Contents page

- Dedication (short, usually to family members or others who inspire you)*

- Foreword (500 words, written by someone else)*

Introduction – 1,500 words

- Who your book is written for

- Who you are

- Why you've written the book

- What your book's big promise is to the reader

Part One* (eg Beginning, Status Quo or Theory)

- Includes 2 to 5 CHAPTERS – Up to 10,000 words

- Each chapter contains 3 to 5 topics, illustrated consistently with case studies, anecdotes, research, references, etc

Part Two* (eg Middle, Main Content or Model)

- Includes 2 to 5 CHAPTERS – Up to 10,000 words

- Each chapter contains 3 to 5 topics, illustrated consistently with case studies, anecdotes, research and references, etc

Part Three* (eg End, Implementation or Outcomes)

- Includes 2 to 5 CHAPTERS – Up to 10,000 words

- Each chapter contains 3 to 5 topics, illustrated consistently with case studies, anecdotes, research and references, etc

Conclusion/Summary – 500 to 1,000 words

- Main points of your book

- What the reader now knows

- What the future holds for them

- What they should do next (contact you, further free info…)

Back matter – 1,000 words

- References/Further Reading*
- Acknowledgements (thank anyone and everyone who has helped get your book inspired, written and published)
- The Author (300-word bio ending with your website, social media contact details and a hi res black-and-white headshot)

*Optional

Total Word Count: *typically, 35,000*

Summary

The two models that will help you plan and structure your perfect business book are:

The PLAN model – Position, Listen, Ambition, Niche Vision – an easy way to write your book's Introduction and ensure you are speaking directly to your ideal client about their central question and offering them your big promise.

The BUILD system, our unique card system either using physical cards or our bespoke software, to structure your book with Basics, Uniques, Inspiration,

Linear and Definition. Don't forget to organise your cards into a linear contents page – your book blueprint – before starting to write your first draft.

With these models, nothing sells you like your book. And no one builds your book like Rethink.

Next, we move onto Part Two – Writing Your Book.

PART TWO
WRITING YOUR BOOK

Now you've positioned your book, have a working title and subtitle in place, and have an Introduction and a detailed contents page based on your BUILD cards, it's time to get down to the writing of 30,000 to 40,000 words. It may well be that your expertise lies predominantly in the subject matter of your book, rather than writing, and that you feel a little daunted by the job that lies ahead. Stick with us. While writing a book is rarely easy, we're going to show you the easiest way to get those words and thoughts out of your head and onto the page. The important thing is to take it step by step and not get overwhelmed by what may feel right now like a massive amorphous task.

5
Preparing To Write

Before you start the writing process, we're going to talk about personalising the AUTHOR framework to your mindset, the idea of doing some research that will make your book unique, and some tips and tools to keep in mind while writing. This chapter will cover:

- Your AUTHOR brain – use our vision framework to pre-set your motivation and mindset

- Two kinds of research that will add substance, content and originality to your manuscript

- Your writing style

- The length of your book

- The 3 Ts of content creation

Your AUTHOR mindset

Remember the AUTHOR framework from Chapter 2, with its Attention, Understand, Trust, Help, Order and Reaction steps? Take some time to review these elements again and make notes on any thoughts that come to you as a result of applying the elements to your well-structured book.

Once you start focusing on these elements, in advance of and while writing your manuscript, you will find yourself in a heightened state of awareness. New ideas will float up from the library of your subconscious – books you read, things people say and the media (social and otherwise) will seem to crackle with relevant facts, figures, information and links.

Writing a book is not just about the time you spend typing at your keyboard with your eyes on your screen (or writing in a notebook, if you prefer old-school tools). It is about all the times in between when your mind is consciously and unconsciously review-ing, sifting, connecting and shaping the knowledge you have into elements of your book. It's a state of mind you enter for the period of the writing process, and an awareness of how to leverage this state of mind will help you create an inspirational book.

It may be a cliché or a well-used metaphor to talk about the two kinds of processing our brains carry out: Buddhism characterises them as intellect and intuition, Carl Jung as conscious and subconscious, Daniel Kahneman as thinking fast and slow. However you want to describe them, we have overt, aware thought-processing that deals with instant problems and questions, does active planning and organising, logical analysis and decision-making, keeps short-term dates and times in mind, and works during your waking hours; and we have covert, opaque concept-processing that carries out more complex functions like meeting deadlines, finding solutions to intractable problems, germinating new ideas, linking events and concepts, retrieving buried information from our mental archive, and 'composting' books and other projects, without our conscious involvement.

When you step into the world of writing your book, you can engage your intuition, subconscious or thinking fast in an active way to expand your thought processes. If you purposefully set your subconscious to work on both general creativity and specific tasks, it will take up the challenge and save you lots of conscious work and hard thinking time.

Use the AUTHOR framework for your own benefit while you write:

- Pay **Attention** to the work your subconscious can do for you by planning ahead. Decide on the subject of a writing session the day before, make a note of the title and tell your subconscious to prepare. You'll be surprised at how much smoother your subsequent writing time is than if you were starting from scratch.

- **Understand** your personal preferences and styles for thinking, planning, organising and meeting deadlines; consciously use your strengths and mitigate any weaknesses for the benefit of this task.

- **Trust** your reticular activating system – the part of your brain that acts as a gatekeeper to your conscious awareness. It protects you from overwhelm by filtering out the unnecessary and less important aspects of life. If you train it to focus on book-related information, you will begin to find that useful information from all sources appears as if by magic in your mental inbox.

- Ask for **Help** when you need it, from those around you at home and at work – you might need them to cut you some slack, especially while you're writing your first draft. And professional help could make the difference between a good book and a great book that will transform your business.

- Maintain **Order** in your thoughts and your writing. Stick to writing from the detailed contents page you made from your BUILD book plan, whether in chronological order or not. Create your writing habit (coming up in Chapter 6) and stick to it. Use your Bookbuilder Planner to plan your work in advance and keep a record of the creative process you're going through.

- Expect the positive **Reaction** your book will earn and the value it will bring to more people than you can imagine. Plan for the constructive effect it will have on your ideal clients and enjoy the unexpected reactions from further afield.

CASE STUDY – *GRANDPA ON A SKATEBOARD* GETS A BIG REACTION

Tim Farmer, author of *Grandpa on a Skateboard*,[12] is a pretty low-key person of influence in his vitally important area of expertise – the assessment and evaluation of an individual's ability to make a decision. The introduction of the Mental Capacity Act (2005) provided health and legal professionals with a framework to assess mental capacity, but in practice mental capacity assessments are often misunderstood and poorly conducted. Tim's *Grandpa on a Skateboard* was the first practical book for health

---

12   Tim Farmer, *Grandpa On A Skateboard: The practicalities of assessing mental capacity and unwise decisions* (Rethink Press, 2016)

ınd legal professionals that simplified and explained the assessment process. Although Tim did very little to promote his book when it came out (social media is not his thing), his use of real-life case studies and clear, jargon-free guidance was so brilliant at demystifying the assessment process that *Grandpa on a Skateboard* spread like wildfire through his market. Six months after launching his book, Tim posted in an entrepreneur group asking for help: his clients had more than doubled, he had a waiting list for his services, and he needed support in building out capacity and systems. A first world problem, for sure, but don't under-estimate the power your book will have to sell you and your business.

Research

You might want to consider increasing or consolidating your unique and original content by doing some primary research on your own market or subject matter. There are two kinds of research:

Quantitative research produces facts, figures and hard data. This comes from 'closed' questions in surveys or questionnaires, meaning the questions are designed to have binary (yes/no, 1/0, tick/cross), multiple choice or numerically ranked answers. You can analyse this data and discuss the results in your text; you can display the results as illustrative 'Inspirations' in bullet pointed lists, percentages, averages, graphs, charts and tables. Closed questions with pre-coded response options are ideal for topics where you know what kinds of responses you want in order to support and illustrate the points you're making in your book.

Quantitative research requires a reasonable number of responses to a survey or questionnaire to make the outcomes and conclusions you can draw from them credible, or 'statistically significant'. There's no fixed number that makes your research statistically significant – it depends on the context and the nature of the sample market you are surveying.

Qualitative research creates personal responses based on experience, beliefs, opinions and behaviour. Qualitative research is extracted from the answers to 'open' questions recorded or written in interviews, focus groups and surveys, where you ask participants to give reasons for or expand their views on a 'closed' response, or as stand-alone questions or discussions. These are perfect for 'Uniques' such as verbatim quotes, case studies or individual examples of numerical data. Remember that if you are going to attribute a real person's name to a quote or reference them in a case study, you will need to show them the exact wording of the content about them and get their written permission to use it. If they don't want to be named or quoted, your alternative is to keep the essence of the content but anonymise or change the details so neither they nor anyone else could recognise them.

Open questions should be used where possible replies are unknown or too numerous to pre-code. Open questions are more demanding for respondents, but if well answered they can provide useful insight into a topic. Open questions can also be time consuming to administer and difficult to analyse. Whether using open or closed questions, researchers should plan clearly how answers will be analysed.

For Lucy's book *A Book of One's Own*, she surveyed fifty women authors, using open and closed questions, and interviewed ten at length. The responses to the survey and the content of the interviews were used as a substantial amount of book content and the interviews were the beginning of her podcast.[13]

Check out the survey at **bit.ly/ABOOSurvey**

Your writing style

The style of writing can make a big difference to the positioning of your book and the impact it has on your

---

13   Lucy McCarraher, 'A Book of One's Own' [podcast] www. abookofonesown.co.uk/a-book-of-ones-own-blog [accessed 8 October 2020]

readers, and therefore on you and your business. First-time writers are often advised to 'write how you speak'. While this idea helps ensure that your text is natural and congruent with the 'real you', if you pasted a chunk of your real-life speech into your book it would seem unfocused, long-winded, boring and would appear – strangely – unnatural. If you've ever tried to read verbatim transcripts of interviews, you'll know how hard they are to plough through. Readers don't want to see in print the ums and ers, pauses, digressions and waffling that makes up everyday chat.

We also all have lazy habits in speech that make for difficult reading when you transfer them to the page. Most of us don't construct our spoken sentences efficiently to get information across in the clearest way. We can rely on our facial expression, body language and context to add meaning to our words while talking directly to someone, but when you're engaging through written material it's 100% words.

For some people, speaking comes more naturally than writing, and it can make sense to 'write' your book by recording and transcribing rather than writing directly. Bear in mind what we said above, though, and realise that you will have an extra task of editing the transcripts back to a simpler and more direct writing style. We recommend rev.com for quick and accurate transcription; otter.ai is a free or cheap – but less accurate – alternative.

If you're a first-time author, you may feel tempted to adopt a writing style that you think gives you more gravitas than the way you would normally communicate. You don't need to do this; in fact, you definitely should not do this, as readers want to feel personally involved with the authentic you, not lectured by some academic or business guru.

Writing that tries to be too clever comes across as self-conscious and the reader will often feel embarrassed by the author's fumbling attempts to impress. Most people read a book firstly because they want the information it contains – or, more specifically, the benefits it promises – and secondly because they believe and trust that the author is someone who can give them that information. If what you're writing is genuine, unambiguous and easy to read, you've given the reader what they want. This is why we suggest you write to a single ideal client, so your author voice feels natural and focused to the perfect reader.

While you don't want to make spelling, punctuation and grammatical errors that will cause irritated readers to post sarcastic reviews on your Amazon page, you shouldn't worry too much about getting it all right – especially in your first draft. In the first instance, concentrate on your message more than the medium. And remember, no book should ever be published without a professional copy editor having worked rigorously through it to weed out any errors the author might have left in.

Lucy was once given the best advice by an editor: 'Be kind to your readers'. It's in your interest for readers to enjoy reading your book and not to feel as though it's hard work to understand or an uphill battle to get through. If there's a hard way or an easy way to say something, use the easy way. If there's a long way or a short way to describe something, take the short route. Avoid technical jargon wherever possible. Do your reader a favour by being crystal clear and by not assuming they have your level of knowledge – they are reading your book precisely because they don't, so make sure your points are easy to understand. If you need to use an obscure word or an acronym, provide a definition or spell it out in full the first time you use it. If you have to use, and they need to learn, special-ist terms, consider including a glossary at the back of the book so they can always look up what they aren't familiar with.

Check out some of the top business or self-help books in any field. Most of them use simple language and construction to tell their stories – which, when done well, is the height of sophistication.

How many words?

The length – use word count as number of pages isn't a useful marker – of your book is important for a number of reasons. First, business or self-help books win over fiction and narrative nonfiction because they can be shorter and yet perceived as (and therefore priced at) higher value. An average novel is 80,000 words, but in paperback it's likely to be priced at under £10. The average business or self-help book is under 40,000 words but likely to be priced at £12 or more.

In our experience, readers of business or self-help titles want a solution to their problem or answer to their question quickly and practically. They want to soak up the information from the book like a sponge, then be able to go and put it into action. They likely won't read a book that would take them several weeks to get through (like a long literary classic or analytical history book), and that means they will never understand your full message or be able to make effective use of it.

We advise you to think in terms of 30,000 to 40,000 words. Some self-help books can be dense but brief, between 20,000 and 30,000 words. A book of 15,000 words or fewer is what we publish as a 'mini book'. A book length of 35,000 words is a safe and workable average that offers enough solid content without making the reader work too hard or too long.

The 3 Ts

The '3 Ts' is known in fiction and drama as the 'three-act structure'; more simply, it involves ensuring that your book – and every section, chapter and sub-section thereof – has a clearly defined beginning-middle-end structure. This particularly applies to each chapter of a business or self-help book, though it should also be used to format shorter pieces, from articles and blog posts to emails and letters.

T1. Tell them what you're going to tell them. Give the big picture and/or set the scene.

T2. Tell them. In the main part of your book/ chapter/article/post, present all the information, adding in the necessary detail, and lead logically from one point to the next. T2 is the substantive part of your piece and may include sections with their own sub-headings.

T3. Tell them what you've told them. Summarise and recap; if appropriate, include a call to action. This could be a succinct paragraph, a bulleted list or a set of exercises; where appropriate, it should lead the reader into the next chapter or section.

Here comes our third T of this chapter – the summary.

Summary

Before you start writing:

- Revisit the AUTHOR framework, which holds you to a gold standard in every aspect of writing your book.

- Be aware that writing your book is an all-consuming process and not just the time you spend actually writing.

- Decide whether you should carry out some quantitative and/or qualitative research that could add substance, content and originality to your manuscript.

- Keep your writing style simple, natural, and addressed to your favourite ideal client and no one else.

- Remember the length of your book should be 40,000 words or under – although the first draft may be longer, especially if you record and transcribe.

- Make sure that every part of the manuscript includes the 3 Ts of content creation.

6
Writing Your First Draft

Now you've completed the planning stages, we're going to work through the process of writing step by step and in detail.

This is another place where many first-time authors lose their way. They may know who their market is, have crafted a brilliant title and worked out what they want to say in what order – but the tasks of writing, checking, re-writing, reviewing and editing become overwhelming and they give up. One of the main reasons is that they fail to see the writing process as a series of distinct steps which need to be taken in a specific order. They try to do too much at once, in the wrong sequence, mixing up tasks, and find themselves bogged down in a chaos from which it can be difficult to emerge.

Writing a book is a series of discrete tasks which, if carried out one by one and in the right order, makes it simple (if not easy!) to create a great business or self-help book. In this chapter, we'll give you an overview of our WRITER process and look in depth at the hardest and most time-consuming step in the process: creating your first draft.

The WRITER process

We developed our WRITER process to take you through a logical and organised writing sequence that keeps you on track and moving through the necessary steps.

Here are the stages we work through:

W – Write (6 weeks)

R – Review (1 week) } Writing

I – Improve (1 week)

T – Test (3 weeks)

E – Edit (2 weeks) } Editing

R – Repeat (as required)

Here is an overview of the **WRITER Process**:

1. **Write**: Your first draft doesn't have to be brilliantly written; it just has to be written. It's probably the hardest part of the entire book-writing process, even though at times it will feel exciting and exhilarating, but it just has to be done. This step is about quantity – 30,000 to 40,000 words; quality is not an issue at this point.

2. **Review**: Don't mistake this step for proofreading or editing; reviewing is looking through your book with the perspective of a reader rather than a writer. Print out and read through your first draft, looking for any gaps, repetitions, inconsistencies or obvious errors, and make notes.

3. **Improve**: With your Review notes, work through your book one chapter at a time, to add, remove, re-order or sharpen content. You can work on your style, too, but this is not your main focus during this step. This is your second draft, but again, it doesn't have to be perfect.

4. **Test:** Get some beta reader feedback on your second draft manuscript. In Chapter 8, we'll tell you how to identify and brief no more than six trusted colleagues, clients, authors, influencers or others who fall within the potential market of your book, to read your draft and give you honest feedback. This step is often left out, but it's essential.

5. **Edit:** Now you get to process all the suggestions made by your beta readers and decide which to implement. Make a plan for structural or major content changes first. Then work through your document slowly, checking each sentence, as well as each paragraph, section and chapter, for sense and structure. This is your final draft.

6. **Repeat:** You may need to revisit some of the steps, particularly 4 and 5, till you feel your final draft is as good as you can make it. Bear in mind, though, that your manuscript will be polished and finalised by a professional editor who will pick up any mistakes you've missed.

Let's go through the steps of the WRITER process in detail.

Step 1: WRITE

The first – and, frankly, hardest – part of writing your book is getting the first draft out of your head and onto the page. Your first draft should be rough and ready; trying to produce a perfect manuscript first time round will waste time and distract you from shaping the basic information into a workable manuscript. Ernest Hemingway is supposed to have said,

'The first draft of anything is shit'.[14] We're not sure about a source for this, but it's a good maxim and almost mandatory. Because you have such a detailed structure for your book, with every topic, case study, anecdote and piece of research listed, you can look at this step as the job of 'writing by numbers' or filling in the gaps – 500 words on this topic, 250 words on that case study, 1,000 words on this aspect of your model.

A good length of time to allocate for writing your first draft is about six weeks. If you let it drag on too long, it may never get finished. When you get into the writing habit, as we'll describe, you should be able to average 1,000 words an hour. If you write at this average speed for one hour a day, six days a week, for six weeks, you'll have written a 36,000-word manuscript.

The WRITE step has three key elements which you will need to establish for yourself in order.

Create a writing schedule

Are you a lark or an owl? Do you feel most energetic, creative and focused in the early mornings, late evenings or some other time? At what point in your day can you most effectively fit your writing appointments into your schedule – and stick to them? When

---

14 Arnold Samuelson, *With Hemingway: A Year in Key West and Cuba* Quote (Random House, 1984), p11 (Verified on paper)

you work on an intensive piece of work like writing your first draft, do you need to break it down into micro-sessions or bite-sized chunks, or stay on task for substantial periods of time?

You need to answer these questions now because mapping out a serious writing schedule for the next six weeks is crucial to getting the job done. For all the hundreds of authors we have mentored through writing their books, the most popular schedule has been to get up an hour early six days a week, head to the writing den, and, without getting waylaid by personal hygiene, emails, social media or anything else, get straight into writing for an hour or so, and then start the rest of their day.

One author used to set the alarm for 4am, write for two hours, return to bed at 6am and get up to a normal day at 8am. A bit extreme, maybe! Another author used to pick two topic cards a day to take everywhere with them. In micro gaps in their schedule – 5 minutes here, 10 minutes there – they would take out their cards and audio record the next several hundred words, noting where they'd got to on the card each time. As someone who could pull focus fast and hold the place they'd got to in their head throughout the day, they got the whole book written like this in six weeks. Others prefer to nap after dinner then write late at night when the rest of the household has gone to bed. And some are able to allocate six entire weekends to writing and get the job done that way.

There's no right or wrong way to schedule the writing of your first draft; whatever works for you is the way to do it. If you find that your initial plans aren't as conducive to getting your first draft written as you imagined, try something different; make whatever adjustments you need to to get the job done.

Whatever schedule you decide on, make it tangible and visible in whatever you use for planning your time: online calendar, paper diary – or, if you're on the Bookbuilder programme, your Bookbuilder Planner. Physically writing in your sessions and seeing them in the context of your other events, meetings, calls and reminders will set them in your mind and make them harder to avoid. Schedule your writing sessions as high-importance events. If you have to miss a scheduled writing session, re-schedule it asap and get back on track.

Make writing a habit

We all know how easy it is to get into bad habits: just do the same thing at the same time in the same way for a few days, and your morning tea break just no longer feels complete without that Mars Bar. Luckily, though, you can use your natural ability to form a positive habit to help get your first draft written.

If possible, decide on a single place where you're going to do all your writing. It might or might not be where you regularly work. Let's call it your writing den. Then, every time you go into your writing den for a writing session, add your writing props – maybe the same mug with the same hot drink (maybe even the same Mars Bar) or the same music track. The more of your senses you engage as triggers, the quicker the habit will become ingrained, so also consider using a particular fragrance, wearing the same clothes...

Sitting down to write at the same time – especially early in the morning – each day may be hard at first, but stick to your scheduled writing times, trying to make them as regular and similar (same place, same time, same props) as possible, and your mind will soon see these as triggers to work and switch into creative mode on cue.

You can get help with sticking to your writing habit from those around you. Tell work colleagues, people at home and even clients that you are writing your first draft over the next six weeks. This way, you make yourself externally accountable for achieving your goal and can ask for support for this limited period of time. Your book, after all, will benefit your company, your family and your market.

Stick to it and don't get side-tracked

This step is called WRITE because that's what it's about. It's not about reading, reviewing, researching, re-writing, editing or proofreading. You won't write your first draft of 30,000 to 40,000 words in six weeks if you do anything other than write.

When you start a writing session, don't begin by re-reading the section you wrote yesterday or checking the spelling and punctuation of an earlier piece. Don't worry about whether you've perfectly expressed your ideas or been as witty as you'd hoped. Just get straight into today's chosen section: write it and then stop. Decide (and note down) the topic for your next session and let your subconscious go to work on it in the meantime. You'll be surprised at how much work your brain has done in the background when you start writing again.

When you're writing and you come to gaps in terms of research, statistics, contributions from others, additional case studies and so on, leave yourself a note to add these in the next step, but don't step away from your manuscript to google the information you want or email someone about an interview, at least not during your writing session. If it helps, keep a running list of the additional content you will need to add to the next draft. This sort of work will be taken care of in the REVIEW and IMPROVE steps. The following procrastination activities can distract you from your task of getting your first draft written:

- Reviewing

- Re-reading

- Formatting

- Checking quotations or facts

- Researching

- Editing

- Talking about your writing

- Worrying about writing or publishing your book

- Checking social media for book-related posts

- Online shopping

Because you've planned your book in such meticulous detail, you don't have to write your first draft in chronological order. If you get stuck on a topic, move on to another one that inspires you more and come back to the other one later. Keep your book blueprint nearby and tick off the sections as you complete them. This will give you a nice dopamine hit each time. Keep each chapter in a separate file at this stage, although you'll need to combine your manuscript into a single Word document at the end.

Be aware that writing – especially your first draft – can be a time of emotional ups and downs. The first 5,000 words may come easily; the next 10,000 may feel much harder. At times you'll feel totally in the flow and that what you're writing is earth-shatteringly brilliant; at other times you'll curse yourself, or us, for getting you into this pointless project because everything you write has been said before and no one will want to read your book. While it's possible that the first mindset is a little overblown, the second is certainly wrong. The important thing to remember is that every author goes through these same mood swings and the only way to deal with them is to step back from your feelings and plough on through. Typically, you'll experience a breakthrough at about 20,000 words: you'll come to a session and suddenly see that you're over the worst, that you've written a serious body of work and there is light at the end of the tunnel. Then you'll be on the downhill run.

Summary

We've introduced you to the WRITER process, and taken you in detail through Step 1:

- WRITE – create your first draft by implementing a writing schedule and a writing habit, and by sticking to it for six weeks while you get the knowledge in your head out and onto the page.

There's more work to come – five more steps – but when you've completed this one, you should feel an enormous sense of satisfaction and congratulate yourself. The hardest part is over!

7
Moving To Your Second Draft

If you've followed the guidance in the last chapter, your first draft manuscript will be complete – and rough and ready. You won't have stopped to review what you've written, corrected your grammar, spelling and punctuation, or even googled the odd statistic or piece of information you need to make a point.

In the next two steps, you'll work through your rough first draft and polish it up into a much more readable second draft. Again, you're not aiming for perfection or a finished manuscript here. After completing these steps, you'll be sending your second draft to beta readers for feedback, and there's no point in perfecting a manuscript that is likely to need further changing. But let's not get ahead of ourselves; the next two steps of the WRITER process that will take you to your second draft are:

- REVIEW – evaluating and annotating the manuscript
- IMPROVE – implementing the changes that take you to the second draft stage

Step 2: REVIEW

If you stick to the same schedule of approximately six hours a week, you can get this step done in one week.

First, make a note of your total word count, and the word count of each chapter. Format your manuscript or individual chapter documents in 12pt Arial, Calibri or Times New Roman font (the easiest fonts to read) with 1.5 line spacing and with each chapter starting on a new page. Don't use any fancy fonts, boxes or grey backgrounds for headings, quotes or breakout boxes at this stage. Then print out the whole manuscript.

Now (and this is genuinely important), take a break from it. Give yourself a day or two away from your first draft and try not to even think about it, let alone look at it.

This is a vital, distinct step in the WRITER process, and one that is often left out or muddled up with proofing and editing. When you take the time to carry out this task on its own before moving onto the next steps, you bring extra clarity to your manuscript, which will show up in the final draft.

When you return to your hard-copy manuscript, you need to change your perspective. A crucial aspect of REVIEWing your work is to step outside your writer mode and into reader mode; this is why you've printed it out. Reading your own words on paper gives you more separation than if you return to what you're used to seeing on the screen. You need as much objectivity and distance as possible to identify where there are gaps, repetitions, inconsistencies or actual errors.

Work through your whole book, slowly and carefully, always with a pen in hand. Try, though, to carry out this task at times that are outside your writing schedule – perhaps times when you would normally read for knowledge, interest or pleasure. For this step, you don't want to trigger your writing habit with its normal place, time and props. Now you're no longer the author but an impartial reader – as far as you can be.

Don't mistake the step of REVIEWing your book for proofreading or editing purposes. This task is not about correcting spelling errors or your grammar (just mark them if you come across any obvious mistakes, but don't make it a focus); it is about assessing whether the structure of your book works – whether your 'story' leads the reader through the information in a logical and compelling way.

Be analytical in your approach and make sure that every point you have made in your first draft follows logically from the previous one. If you're not sure how well a chapter or section works, leave a note to remind yourself to try switching paragraphs or sentences around when you get to the IMPROVE step. Also note your own responses – where you've found a section enjoyable and engaging, and equally where you've been bored, where the text goes on too long or digressed, or where you've found yourself disengaged as a reader.

If your total word count is greater than what you planned or wanted, mark up where you can trim or cut elements. If any of your chapters is markedly longer or shorter than the others, look especially hard for ways to reduce or increase their content.

As you read, check:

- The overall structural integrity and consistency.

- That everything flows logically – is your Framework or Model working?

- Are your chapters and sections roughly the same length?

- Have you introduced and summarised each chapter?

- Do you have enough case studies, anecdotes and other Uniques?

- What other research do you need to do?

- What needs cutting?

Remember: don't make changes while you are REVIEWing, just make notes.

By the time you've REVIEWed the full manuscript, it should be covered in your notes, and you may have some additional pages with more details. At this point, you might want to collate your notes into an articulated critique, particularly about any bigger issues you have become aware of, such as structural problems, gaps and loose ends that still need tying in – anything that feels unsatisfactory or took you out of the reader journey.

Once you have done this, your REVIEW is complete, and you are ready to move on to the next step.

Step 3: IMPROVE

Because you have such detailed notes from your REVIEW work, you'll be able to IMPROVE your manuscript, and get from first to second draft, in another week.

Switch back into writer mode (and writing schedule and habit) and return to your electronic manuscript with your paper notes by your side.

Once again, bear in mind that we haven't yet got to the editing/proofreading stage of the WRITER process, so don't get bogged down in details of spelling or punctuation. Take the biggest issues that your REVIEW has highlighted and work on these first.

If you have found issues with the structure of your book, deal with them first, particularly if an overhaul of the objective or message of the book is in order. Don't be disheartened by the prospect of substantial reworking; even if you need to take some processing time before getting down to it, the solution will become clear, and if you address structural issues at this stage rather than later in the WRITER process your book will be the better for it.

You might have decided that a complete chapter is in the wrong place and needs moving, or that sections within one or more of the chapters should be re-ordered. If you move chapters or sections, remember to check all other references to this content throughout the rest of the book, and review the chapter or section holistically again when you have finished.

After that, sorting out the smaller concerns of filling gaps in content, carrying out additional research, trimming material or sharpening up the presentation of your ideas will clarify the content in your own mind as well as in those of your readers.

Your REVIEW may have shown you that your authorial voice wasn't quite how you want to come across to your readers. Were there places where you became overly technical when you are writing for a non-professional market? Alternatively, did you over-explain in a way that might seem patronising to a readership well versed in your area of expertise?

Although this isn't your final edit, try to improve any areas where your writing voice didn't feel right in your review. You may not have got into your writing stride until two or three chapters in, so check that your early chapters have the same feel – where you comfortably talk to your ideal client – as the later ones.

CASE STUDY – WORLD-CHAMPION CYCLIST TO BESTSELLING AUTHOR

Neil Fachie, multiple-world-champion cyclist, Paralympian and world-record holder, had never seen himself as a writer. He had written the occasional blog post, but nothing more. Working through the planning strategies with Lucy, he could see a clear path and suddenly writing his book seemed to be a reality. The writing process itself had its challenges for Neil, especially as he is partially sighted, and he says he developed a love/hate relationship with his manuscript. But the steps of the WRITER process allowed him to see it develop incrementally, until he felt confident enough to submit his 'baby' to Rethink Press. He admits it was a little daunting. He worried about what the editors would think – would they rip it to shreds? Far from it. The WRITER process had worked, the professional editors clearly knew their stuff and, most importantly, cared about Neil's book. Neil Fachie's *Earn Your Stripes* became an Amazon #1 bestselling title and has promoted his methodology for enhancing performance in business and life to a wider audience.[15]

When you've done your best to fix your big-picture issues, work through the manuscript from start to finish, correcting every point you've noted from your review and anything else that shows up as you progress.

---

15   Neil Fache, *Earn Your Stripes: Gold medal insights for business and life* (Rethink Press, 2020)

Keep an eye out for consistency as you IMPROVE the second draft of your business or self-development book. Ensure that your chapters are all a similar (but not necessarily identical) length, that the sections within each chapter are similarly divided up and that the chapters are all structured in the same way. Each chapter must start with some kind of introduction and end with a summary. These could be short paragraphs, bullet points or, for the summary, some short exercises or checklists that show the reader what they've learned.

The IMPROVE step is also a good time to make your manuscript as reader friendly as possible because the next step is to TEST it with beta readers. If you've been working in individual chapter documents, you now need to pull them all into a single Word document, formatted as specified in the REVIEW step.

At the end of Step 3, you will have created a much-improved second draft of your self-help book, making it ready for the next step, TEST. The TEST step takes you into the editing phase.

Summary

In this chapter we've worked through the second and third steps of the WRITER process, which have taken you through a first self-edit, polishing your first draft to create your second draft manuscript.

- REVIEW – where you've worked through a hard-copy version of your first draft as an objective reader, marking up the good, the bad and the ugly, so it's ready to upgrade to a second draft.

- IMPROVE – the process of implementing the changes you noted in your printed manuscript, revising structure and content where necessary, adding the missing elements and refining areas that were overlong, repetitive or off track.

8

Finalising Your Manuscript

I n this chapter we discuss taking your second draft manuscript and showing it to a select group of beta readers to get the essential feedback you need, as an author, before submitting your book to a publisher and getting a professional edit. Too many authors think they can skip this step, which means that instead of getting private, personalised scrutiny from the people who matter that they can incorporate into their final self-edit, they can get public negative feedback like poor reviews on Amazon.

To make sure that your final draft is as good as it can be before the professionals start work, we'll give you the last three steps of the WRITER process, and throw in some writing tips for good measure. We'll be working through:

- The TEST step – selecting and briefing the right beta readers so you get the right feedback

- The EDIT step – incorporating the beta readers' feedback into a final draft of your manuscript

- The REPEAT step – going back over any steps you need to

- The Foreword to your book

- Formatting, referencing and submitting your manuscript

Step 4: TEST

Having written a second draft of your manuscript in the IMPROVE step, you are now going to TEST your book on a select readership. You've written a first draft, stood back from your manuscript to review it and then improved your book as much as you can for the moment. Now the most important thing you can do is ask a few trusted individuals to give you their honest opinions. This is not a task you should be employing professionals for, or offering payment to anyone.

Choosing your beta readers

Who should you ask to be a 'beta reader' for your book? Your choice is important and will affect the quality of the feedback you receive. Ideal candidates are all people you know, like and trust, and should include:

- **A colleague or two** who know your subject matter in at least the same depth as you. They can tell you how well you have covered the material, where you have gaps to fill or if you have made any factual errors. These might be people you work with or work separately from, but a serious competitor probably isn't the right person for this job.

- **Trusted clients, customers or prospects** (two or three, max) who represent the target market (ideal client) of your book, and who will give you valuable insight into how well you engage your readers and offer them practical solutions to the problems they experience in your niche area.

- **A key person** in your industry who you feel comfortable approaching for this favour. Don't worry about imposing on them; people are usually flattered to be asked their opinion of a book manuscript, and this person may be someone who could write you a Foreword – or at least a praise quote – if they like what they read, and feel invested enough to promote your book in your market.

- **A reader of business books** whose opinion you trust and who doesn't necessarily specialise in your subject matter. It's worth asking this person whether, even if your book isn't one they would normally choose to read, it's still of general interest and structured and written well enough to hold the attention of a 'lay' person. If they read a variety of books, you might get some disinterested objective feedback that you wouldn't get from others.

We suggest you do *not* ask family or friends to act as beta readers at this stage. They will be inclined to give you only the good news, which may be what you would like but is not what you need to hear. They are unlikely to be your target market or subject experts, and their judgement of your writing will almost certainly be skewed. Equally, some friends will find it challenging to accept you as an author, might feel jealous and might (even unconsciously) deliver negative feedback that says more about their personal reaction than the quality of your book.

Working with your beta readers

You'll need to give your beta readers a deadline for reviewing your manuscript; two to three weeks should be long enough if you give them clear instructions and a manuscript in the format they're most comfortable with. For best results, contact your beta readers well in advance and give them as accurate timings as possible for when you will deliver the manuscript and the deadline for receiving their feedback. Make sure they've booked this job into their schedule and don't try to put it off at the last minute.

Also ask your beta readers how they would like to read your manuscript – electronically or in hard copy. If it's the latter, supply your beta readers with a tidy, printed copy of your manuscript and ask them to read it with a pen in hand. Some will prefer it loose leaf; for others it's worth getting a bound copy if it makes the task easier for them. For those who are happier with an electronic copy, send them a Word document and make sure they know how to use the Review function so they can make suggestions inline and/or with comments in the margin.

Be clear with them about what sort of feedback you want from them: it must be honest, specific and constructive, including positive reactions as well as improvements they think you could make. Request politely that they get the job done by your agreed deadline. Make sure they know this is a draft and unedited manuscript, and that you do *not* want them to correct your spelling, punctuation or grammar as that will be done later by a professional editor.

Ask them to tell you:

- Their overall reaction – and especially whether they wanted to read on to find out what you were going to say next.

- What they thought the book was going to teach them and whether it lived up to their expectations.

- Whether they were entirely clear about what you were telling them all the time. Ask them to mark sections where they felt lost or confused and to explain why.

- Whether they found it easy to read – in the sense of not being distracted by poor grammar, spelling, punctuation, hard-to-follow information or instructions (bearing in mind that this is only your second draft).

- Where they got bored, felt you were going on too long or found that you were repeating yourself.

- Whether there were any obvious gaps or inconsistencies.

- What they enjoyed most.

- What they would most like you to change.

While your manuscript is away with beta readers, now might be a good time to write any of the additional pages you haven't yet written. In the publishing trade, we call these pages **front matter** and **back matter**. To recap what we described in the 'Your contents page' section in Chapter 4:

FRONT MATTER:

- Praise quotes – no more than 12, and they must be about the book, not you or your business or services.

- Dedication – very short, usually to family members or other inspiration to you.

- Foreword, written by someone else – a big or reputable name in your industry, ideally. It may be that one of your beta readers writes your Foreword, or that you want to send the manuscript to the writer after it has been professionally edited.

BACK MATTER:

- Bibliography / Further Resources
- Acknowledgements – anyone and everyone who has helped get your book inspired, written and published
- The Author page – 200-300 words, ending with your website and social media contact details,

and accompanied by a hi res black and white headshot of you

This is also the time to identify contacts, experts and thought leaders in your field whose support on publication could be useful, and who, if they like your book, you could ask to write a short recommendation. Some of these will be your beta readers, but you might want to ask beyond that group. You can use their short recommendation paragraphs (three to four sentences) on a 'Praise' page at the front of the book, a couple of single-sentence quotes on the cover, and you can also use the testimonials in marketing and PR.

Remember to thank all your beta readers in your Acknowledgements section at the end of the book.

When you get the feedback from your beta readers, enjoy the positives, but accept any negative responses from honest readers at this stage as a gift; they may save you from rejection from publishers, a poor reception from your prospects, or bad reviews from your critics or paying readers.

When your beta readers have given you their feedback, you will have the information you need to carry out the next step, EDIT.

Step 5: EDIT

Take a final two weeks to complete your final self-editing process before handing your manuscript to your publisher or editor. It's easy to feel there's always more you can do to improve your final manuscript, but most authors get to the point where they can't see the wood for the trees and more tweaking doesn't improve anything. You'll be amazed when you get your copy-edited manuscript back how an objective professional can give the final polish to all your hard work.

Only at this point, with all the notes and critiques from your beta readers, will you have an idea of the size and complexity of your editing task. Whether your structure hangs together but your style and grammar need another look, or whether you realise that an overhaul of some sections is required, don't be daunted.

First collate all your feedback. It might not all be consistent; your readers may disagree with each other and take different points of view. Take seriously anything that two or more of readers do agree on. Try to assess criticism objectively, even though you would rather listen to the praise. Decide which suggestions you are going to accept and implement – in the end, this is your book, and you're under no obligation to do what your beta readers suggest.

Be systematic

It is crucial to be systematic when editing. Stop thinking like a writer and try to take on the mindset of a professional editor. This means stepping back from your book and looking for what might be missing, such as a crucial step, a case study or a key piece of information in the right place. Is there too much personal opinion or too much focus on your own experience? Or too little of you personally in the book? Are the quotes and case studies furthering your message or getting in the way? Be systematic – and ruthless.

Big picture, then the detail

As with previous steps in the WRITER process, work from the wider structural issues first, through the chapter-by-chapter changes, and then, once you have resolved any big issues, it's time to go through the manuscript a second time and edit for fine detail.

Tighter writing

If there's one thing that defines a professional writer, it's the tautness of their prose style. Amateur writers' sentences often meander, twist and turn; they use more words than required; and they over-complicate their syntax in an effort to sound sophisticated. Your copy editor will work on this for you, but anything you can do in advance of their work will help them and make the book feel more like your own.

To keep your writing tight, check – on a sentence-by-sentence basis – whether you have used the shortest, simplest word necessary for your meaning; that every word in each sentence is necessary; that all your verbs are active and direct (passive verbs sound pompous and long-winded); and cut out any unnecessary adjectives, adverbs or qualifiers (such as 'rather', 'very', 'quite'). Twenty words is a good average length for a sentence.

In addition to checking for tighter writing, paragraph and sentence construction, make sure you:

- Check your facts – dates, science, events, numbers, people's names, and accurate and referenced quotations.

- Vary your vocabulary and sentence structure – try not to use the same word more than once in a paragraph; find different ways to express yourself.

- Read aloud for rhythm – if any sentence doesn't feel right, read it aloud to discover where it's losing pace or tying itself in knots.

Step 6: REPEAT

We've reached the final step of the WRITER process for getting your book written and edited to a high standard. So far you have Written, Reviewed, Improved, Tested and Edited your manuscript – at which point it may seem as though you have done enough.

The final step is optional and depends on whether you feel the need to REPEAT the last two steps to bring your book even closer to perfection.

Having given your book a final self-edit and incorporated the feedback you've chosen to implement from your beta readers, some authors find it useful to ask one or more of their beta readers to give the manuscript another pass.

At this stage, you may have initially submitted your manuscript to your publisher and they asked you to make a few more changes before it's ready to go into their production process, which will usually start with a copy-edit.

The Foreword to your book

Often misunderstood, and sometimes misspelled (as 'forward' or 'foreward'), a Foreword is a useful – though not essential – part of your book. It sets the stage for you, the author, and, if written by someone with a well-known or often-searched name, it can boost marketing and sales of your book.

The Foreword lets the reader know in a short summary what the book is about and why it is significant. It can contextualise and sell the book and you, the author, from an objective but knowledgeable point of view.

Who writes the Foreword?

Not you, the author! You write your own Introduction, but the Foreword writer should be an experienced and qualified person in your or a related industry or market, or simply someone well known whose name helps validate the work and endorse the expertise of you as the author.

What should they say?

Some Forewords are short – as little as 200 words – but 500 to 1,000 words is ideal.

The writer of the Foreword should think in terms of engaging the reader quickly. It should start with an intriguing hook – a question or statement that grabs attention and introduces the subject matter.

In the subsequent paragraphs, the Foreword should:

1. Set the context in which the Foreword writer knows about the market and its problems, and it should give a personal/professional connection to the subject of the book. It's a good place for the writer to blow their own trumpet subtly; it's one of the payoffs for writing a Foreword for someone else's book, but it's a win-win for them and for you.

2. Summarise the market's (readers') central problem or question (the reason why they picked up or bought the book) and the author's big promise (their solution to the market's question provided in the book).

3. Explain how the Foreword writer knows the author and their expertise in this field. It should emphasise how well the author does what they do (outside the book, in their business) and therefore how qualified the author is to write this book.

4. Highlight some specific content, areas or solutions in the book, as a 'teaser' to the reader, and talk about specific benefits the book will bring to the reader.

5. End with a big plug for the book and its author, and sign off with the Foreword writer's name, credentials or title/company, the title of a recent book (if they have written one) and perhaps their website URL.

Manuscript submission guidelines

When you have come to the end of your own editing abilities, it is time for your publisher to get your manuscript copy-edited, which should include structural comments on your manuscript. As any successful author knows, quality editing is always worth the investment.

To ensure that the publishing process starts with a manuscript that is ready for the best possible professional edit, we send the following formatting guidelines to our authors as a final checklist before they submit their manuscript to us.

What your manuscript should include

- Title page with title, subtitle and author's name

- Contents page

- Praise quotes (optional)

- Dedication (optional)

- Foreword by another person (optional)

- Introduction by the author (approximately 1,500 words)

- Short introduction and conclusion to each chapter

- End-of-book summary (500 to 1,000 words)

- References / bibliography (optional)
- Resources / further reading (optional)
- Acknowledgements
- Author bio

References

You must provide references for all quotes and sources, including:

- All quoted or paraphrased text from printed sources (eg books, journals or magazines) or from online sources, including social media
- Mention of other people's work, processes, concepts, models, etc
- Data or statistics that you have not gathered yourself
- All illustrations that are not your own (whether from printed or online sources)
- All personal communication or other unpublished material (eg interviews)

It's much easier if you source and provide all the references when you submit your manuscript so we don't have to ask you for them during the production process and risk delaying your book's publication.

You will need to show written permission from the copyright holder if you want to reproduce:

- Quoted material that is longer than two short sentences

- Illustrations that are not your own (whether from printed or online sources)

- Epigraphs (inspirational quotes)

- Recognisable details of clients / companies / individuals used in case studies, interviews or other descriptions (changing names alone is not enough to anonymise them)

You can avoid having to get copyright permissions by:

- Using epigraphs (inspirational quotes) that are out of copyright (in the UK, copyright expires seventy years after the author's death)

- Paraphrasing material rather than using verbatim quotes (you still need to provide a reference if you paraphrase)

- Providing your own illustrations (you still need to provide a reference if they are based on someone else's work)

- Leaving out or substantially changing the details of any case studies or mentions of individuals or companies to make them unrecognisable *to themselves or to others*

Formatting your manuscript

Like most publishers, we can only accept manuscripts in MS Word format. If you're a Mac user, you will need to download the full MS Office suite, including Word for Mac. If you've written your book in other software, such as Scrivener, you will still need to format it in Word after outputting it as a Word document.

Font (typeface) and spacing

Please use just one of the following fonts for all body text:

- Times New Roman
- Arial
- Calibri

Whichever one you use, it should be:

- 12pt size
- Aligned left
- Black throughout

- 1.5 line spacing

Use italics for emphasis (sparingly), book or film titles, and non-English words.

Please don't use CAPITALS or **bold** for emphasis – or ***bold italics***, come to that.

Don't try and format 'special' text (eg case studies); just tag and leave a comment like 'Case Study', or write 'Case Study starts' at the beginning and 'Case Study ends' at the end.

Headings and page breaks

- If your book has 'parts' (eg Part One, Part Two...) with several chapters within each part, insert a page break before and after every section/part heading.
- Insert a page break at the start of every chapter.
- Please make sure all your chapter headings are in the same size and style.
- Please make sure all your main sub-headings within chapters are in the same size and style (but different to the chapter headings).
- If you can use Word styles to style your headings, that would be great. Chapter numbers and titles should be Heading 1; main sub-headings within

chapters should be Heading 2. (But if this means nothing to you, don't worry!)

- Please avoid using more than three heading levels.

Summary

This chapter has taken you through the second half of the WRITER process, showing you how to get beta reader feedback and edit your manuscript into a final writer's draft, ready for submission to a publisher and professional copy-editing. We've given you some tips on tighter writing and how to finalise your manuscript in terms of formatting and referencing. In this chapter, we've covered:

- TEST – you've selected and briefed the right beta readers so you get the right feedback

- EDIT – you know how to incorporate their feedback into a final draft of your manuscript

- REPEAT – go back over any of the WRITER process steps if needed

- Tightening your writing, like a true professional

- How to brief the writer of your Foreword

- How to format your manuscript for submission to a publisher

PART THREE
PUBLISHING YOUR BOOK

Now you've been through the hard graft of positioning, planning, writing and editing your book, you need to get it out to your market and the wider world through one of the publishing options available to you. In Part Three, we'll discuss those options and the pros and cons of each one.

9
Traditional And DIY Publishing

U p till about twenty years ago and the emergence of print-on-demand (POD) and online book retailers, there was only one credible route to getting a book published: a contract from what we now call a 'traditional' publishing house. They were the gate-keepers to distribution channels and the only retail outlets, bookstores.

There is no longer any barrier to getting your book in print and selling via the same channels as the traditional publishers. With the barriers down, though, authors need to make informed choices about which route will best suit their needs, and there are positives and negatives to all of them. In this chapter, we'll describe the two best-known publishing options available to you:

- Traditional publishing
- DIY self-publishing

The traditional publisher

Traditional publishers include the big-name, international publishers that everyone has heard of, often known as 'The Big Five' (depending on who has taken over whom lately). Each one owns a range of imprints devoted to different types of fiction and nonfiction, including business and self-help books. There are also a wide range of smaller, independent traditional publishers, several with their own niches in nonfiction and business or self-help publishing.

With the 'traditional' publishing business model, the publisher contracts the author to publish their book. The contract may include the publisher buying the copyright of the author's intellectual property for a defined period of time, which may limit the author's freedom to use their material for other purposes. The publisher may – though this is a diminishing practice – pay the author an 'advance': money in advance of publication that will be recouped by the publisher from the author's royalties from sales. Many authors never actually earn their advance back – in other words, the only money they ever see is the advance, which, unless they are a famous author or celebrity, on an hourly rate of payment for their work is probably under minimum wage. Paying advances which are not recouped is a financial drain for traditional publishers, so increasingly only big-name authors are receiving them.

A big traditional publisher is likely to pay an author 8% to 10% of net receipts from sales of their book (after production, printing and distribution costs, and less the discount payable to wholesalers and retailers); this can be as little as 20p from the sale of an average-priced book. Smaller publishers, especially those who only use POD distribution (more on this shortly), may pay a higher royalty.

The traditional publisher then takes all the financial responsibility for getting the book published, usually including editing, design, typeset, cover design and printing. Traditional publishers, as well as publishing through online retailers like Amazon, will typically produce an 'up front' print run of the book (usually between 1,000 and 3,000 copies – or more if you're an established author with a sales track record) from an offset litho printer and distribute it through physical bookstores. This, however, is becoming increasingly expensive and is often only profitable for well-known authors or other best-sellers where publishers can invest in in-store merchandising (either paid for directly or by offering a discount). The bigger publishers can use their high-selling books to subsidise the distribution of new authors, but smaller traditional publishers may choose not to risk funding the print and distribution costs of a new author's book.

Distributing a book through online retailers is often done through Print On Demand (POD). This is a digital printing process through which small print runs (as low as one copy at a time) can be produced at a reasonable price, as they are ordered by purchasers. While the quality of POD books can be slightly lower than offset litho (traditional) printed books, POD technology and costs are improving all the time. POD allows publishers to avoid risking money on printing books in advance of sales and cuts down the risk of having unsold stock returned or pulped.

Apart from the cost of print, storage and shipping, selling books through physical bookstores is scarcely profitable for publishers, and therefore authors, because retailers often insist on stocking titles on 'sale or return'. Any unsold books will not be paid for, and they must be returned to the publisher at their own expense or simply destroyed. Mainstream publishers typically give a book three months in bookstores before giving up hope of making further sales. If the book doesn't perform well, they abandon the marketing and distribution to focus on new titles, and the author's book is sold for pennies (often less than the physical cost to produce it) or destroyed.

Traditional publishing is most effective for authors who are already well known in their fields, have a big following and a broad-market subject, and will benefit from the kudos of being associated with a specific publishing company. Although landing a big-name publishing contract is the dream for many aspiring authors, being published with a mainstream traditional publisher is not always ideal for entrepreneur authors.

The pros of traditional publishing

Kudos: For many authors the cachet of being taken on by a well-known publishing house is key to their strategy, and such a publisher's backing can translate into a higher media profile, higher fees and a better shot at fame.

Distribution: Your book (at least for a limited time) is more likely to find its way onto bookstores' shelves than it would be using other publishing options. Although being on a shelf in a bookshop amongst loads of other books is no guarantee of success (especially as more sales are going online), it is likely you will make more actual sales (though not necessarily more profit).

Marketing: All big, and some small, traditional publishers have in-house marketing and publicity departments which are there to support authors. They can get great PR coverage for the right book, but all publishers, even the biggest, will only contract a book by an author with a big social media following, who gives talks and workshops where books can be sold, and who has a good marketing plan for their book. They will require the author to work hard to promote themselves and their book to create a maximum number of sales. Traditional publishers look for authors who sell books.

Focus: A traditional publisher takes on the project management of getting your book published, allowing you to concentrate on the main job of writing your next book.

Risk aversion: If you're risk averse or don't have money to spare, a traditional publishing contract with a traditional publisher means you won't have to spend any money on the production of your book – and if you're lucky or famous, they may even give you an advance. However, given the level of competition for publishing contracts, many authors choose to pay for a professional edit *before* submitting their manuscript to an agent or publisher.

The cons of traditional publishing

Loss of freedom: When you work for a publisher (because that's what your contract will mean), some of your creative freedom and your freedom of speech will be quelled. The publisher will need to ensure your book fits their brand and they'll have their own (often good, though sometimes not) ideas about how the book should look, what it will be called, what it should be about and how it should be positioned. Many contracts will also include a clause in the contract saying how long you've got to complete your manuscript. Failing to meet the deadlines imposed by your publisher can result in you losing your contract and your advance.

Loss of control: A traditional publisher may limit what you can do with your book, your use of the book content in other media, such as a course or workshop, or even what you can say about your book. You may need to get approval for a marketing or advertising campaign you'd like to run, and your ability to write another book with another publisher (or even to self-publish) may be subject to certain conditions in your contract. You may think you're only signing over rights to one book, but you could end up signing over your future work too.

Loss of ownership: Many large publishers will stipulate that they own the rights to your work in other languages, territories and formats. Be careful what you're signing and ensure you know your rights. You could end up watching your publisher get rich while you remain unrewarded.

Lack of marketing: The average mainstream publisher organises distribution, puts your book in their catalogue and puts out a press release. These days, as an author, and whichever way you publish your book, marketing and promotion is 100% your job. Even if you're a big-name celebrity or your last book was a best-seller (which you will have had to work hard to promote), your publisher still won't be able to do the interviews or manage your social media for you. You have to be the spokesperson for your book, and that means you need to hustle and be adept at social media. You may even find your publisher, in the interests of protecting their reputation, will ask you to run your own marketing plans by them first.

Loss of profit: As the publisher has taken all the financial risk to get your book published, you will be paid the 'mouse's share' of the proceeds from your book sales. If you have used an agent (often the only way to get your book to a big publisher), you will have to give 10% to 15% of your income to them. In fact, the publisher will pay your agent, who will pay you after they've taken their fee. Trying to land a good agent can be just as difficult as landing a publishing deal. Agents add an additional layer of time, control and cost to your publication.

Loss of time and opportunity: Until you start selling books, the whole process is still a 'cost-money' exercise; you could spend more money and time chasing a publishing contract or agent than if you just self-published. And in that time, who knows how many opportunities you may have missed?

Lack of speed: Publishing behemoths are full of talented people, but the organisations themselves are slow, cumbersome and full of political, financial and shareholder pressures. This all leads to a long delay between landing a deal and selling any books. In addition to the time spent courting and signing with a traditional publisher, it typically takes at least a year from delivering your manuscript for your book to be out and selling.

Expensive author copies: The traditional publishers' business model is based on exploiting the IP published in your book, so their aim is to maximise profit on books sold. This also applies to author copies. If you're an entrepreneurial author and are planning to give books away to build a list or sell direct at events and seminars, expect traditional publishers to offer you only a small discount on your author copies, even if you're ordering thousands.

DIY self-publishing

Authors have been self-publishing their books for hundreds of years, but the advent of digital printing, or POD, and online self-publishing platforms in the 21st century now enables any author who chooses to publish their own book to directly access the same market as traditional publishers. Many self-publishing authors take this route, not as a last resort but because they can make more income per retail sale than a traditional publisher allows them, and because managing the whole publishing process themselves is a cheaper and more hands-on option than hybrid publishing.

DIY self-publishing can look like an attractive publishing option financially, but it involves an author becoming a micro publisher – and the business of publishing, from production of a good book to getting it distributed worldwide, is much more complex than it might appear. If you are not technically knowledgeable, prepared to put in a lot of time learning how to do it properly, or reluctant to pay other professionals to help you publish, you will need to think carefully about this option.

'Self-publishing' is in fact a misnomer. No single individual can carry out all the functions that are required for a book to read, look and feel professional, and to get full distribution through the complicated systems and databases that make up the global book distribution system.

Self-publishing is most effective for fiction or serial authors whose books are their products (rather than sales tools for their businesses), who prefer to keep control of their own publishing process, and for whom learning the intricacies of the publishing industry is worthwhile.

The pros of self-publishing

Freedom, control and ownership: Your book is your own, and no publisher can tell you what they want in it, how it should look and where it should be positioned. You can do whatever you like with your own material: write it as you want it to appear, repackage it in different formats, give some away free…

Maximum profit: All the financial risk in getting your book published has been yours, and the work in getting it distributed has been yours, so 100% of your profit from sales comes directly to you.

Time and opportunity: You are working to your own timescales – on the one hand, you have no deadlines, unless you set them yourself; on the other, you are not waiting on other people's input and schedules. You can take as long or as short a time as you like to write, get the other aspects of publishing sorted out, and spend as much or as little time as you choose on marketing and promotion.

Low risk: You can spend comparatively little, if you so choose, on professional editing, cover design, interior design and typeset, proofreading, e-book conversion, setting up your distribution and printing your own copies. If you have time to spend on learning the publishing ropes that wouldn't be better spent making money in your own area of expertise, you have nothing to lose.

The cons of self-publishing

Lower kudos or reputational damage: In some areas there is still lower status associated with a self-published book, especially if your book appears amateurish in its content or production values. The problem with self-publishing is that unless you have done it multiple times, you don't know what you don't know and your book is almost certain to have some sub-standard elements. If your book is badly written, and I'm afraid to say many self-published books are, you could be doing your reputation more harm than good by having your book out there.

Distribution: You will not be able to get as comprehensive a listing with the databases, printers and wholesalers, who service online and physical bookstores, if you are not a professional publisher with a list of at least ten books and additional subscriptions to their services.

Project management: Unless you pay someone else to manage the process for you, every aspect of the publication of your book is down to you. For a decent result, you must locate and engage professional specialists like editors and designers, manage and coordinate their input, be sure that they have done the job required to the right standard, and also learn the technical side of book production, publishing, distribution and marketing.

Lack of marketing: Even more than with any kind of publisher, as a self-published author marketing and promotion is 110% your job. You have to be the social marketer, PR agent and spokesperson for your book, and that means hustling.

Hidden costs: It is possible to self-publish an e-book at little cost to you, but an e-book alone (or a book published in any single format) is not going to transform your business and your influence in your market. To produce a professional e-book and print book, you will need to pay an experienced editor and cover designer; a typesetter will also make the interior of your book look attractive and more readable than you can; and converting a professional typeset to various e-book formats will also involve the services of a skilled professional.

Technical know-how: In addition to all the know-how required to self-publish, including buying ISBNs, choosing POD or print-then-sell approaches, billing and accounting, you will also need many (often disparate) skills, such as editing, graphic design, typesetting and proofreading. Unless you have all these skills, the only way to do a good job is to pay experts. This increases your outlay, and, as you're responsible for every aspect of the final product, if you get it wrong you may have to pay again. It's not unheard of for self-publishing projects to go way over budget and take inordinate lengths of time when authors take a piecemeal approach.

Post-publication hassle: Deciding to self-publish means you're taking the decision to become a publisher. This business involves additional hassles, including invoicing, chasing payment, sending books for legal deposit (a legal requirement in the UK and other countries), shipping to distributors or customers, specific publishing insurance, collating royalty information for tax purposes and much more.

Summary

The two best-known and most popular routes to publication are:

1. Traditional publishing

2. DIY self-publishing

They each have their pros and cons: traditional publishing works best for well-known authors with big followings and broad-market subjects; self-publishing is most effective for serial fiction or popular non-fiction authors for whom their books are their business and product.

10
Hybrid Publishing

There have been several terms for the kind of publishing that offers a bridge between traditional publishing and self-publishing, including supported publishing, paid-for publishing and partnership publishing. Some hybrid publishers miscall themselves 'self-publishing companies', which is a contradiction in terms. Either the author or the publisher owns a book's ISBN and is therefore the publisher of the book. If the publisher owns it, they have published the book and the author has not self-published. If author owns the ISBN, a company that has provided their publishing services is just that – a publishing services company – and not their publisher.

The business book publishing industry, and its authors, especially in the UK, have now converged on the term 'hybrid publishing' to describe a publishing contract where the author pays a professional publishing company for the costs associated with producing their book – such as editing, design and typesetting, proofreading, cover design, ISBN, e-book conversion, uploading to printers, wholesale and retail distribution, royalty collection/calculation, and ongoing trouble-shooting – and the publisher pays the author a more generous royalty than they would receive through traditional publishing.

This is what we've been doing at Rethink Press since 2011.

Our many authors, and those who have published with other hybrid publishers, choose not to jump through the hoops of chasing a traditional publishing contract, with the uncertainty of ever gaining a contract and the inevitable delays even if they did. Neither do they wish to spend time learning the technicalities of publishing for themselves, nor source and manage the range of individual professionals whose input they would need to self-publish. They want their books published professionally in a short timeframe to underpin their platform of niche expertise, and they want to work with publishing industry experts, enabling them to focus on developing their core business during the publishing process and transforming their business with the excellent book that results.

In some publishing circles, the concept of paid-for publishing is still tarred with the brush of the legacy practice of 'vanity publishing'. Before the advent of POD and online booksellers, anyone who wanted to publish their own book had to do it using so-called vanity publishers. These companies made a portion of their money by persuading hapless authors, often of autobiographies and personal memoirs as well as novels and information books, to pay for big print runs of their book. The authors would then have to store many copies (sometimes thousands) of these volumes, with no means of distributing them other than gifts/sales to family and friends, or paid advertising. Unsurprisingly, vanity publishers earned themselves a bad name (literally) and a bad reputation. Traditional publishers and traditionally published authors looked down on self-published authors as not having written a good enough book to be accepted by a 'real' publisher.

With self-published books, in print and e-book format, now selling as well as traditionally published books, this is (mostly) no longer the case. The Business Book Awards has helped to create a level playing field in the perceptions of different routes to publishing by accepting and encouraging submissions from every kind of publisher, and the knowledgeable and diverse judging panel has picked winners who have published through a range of means.

Reputable hybrid publishing companies should be entirely transparent about their costs and contracts and provide authors with only the services they need and want. There are some 'self-publishing companies', both large and small, that continue the ethos of the original vanity publishers: make money at all costs, especially at the author's cost, in every possible way. This can involve providing poor services at high cost, over-selling and under-performing, selling services such as marketing and promotion as certain ways to sell books when such claims are rarely justified, and outsourcing the services to minimally qualified (and probably poorly remunerated) 'associates'. Most Big Five traditional publishers, having realised the value of the paid-for publishing business model, now use one particular over-sized company to provide the services for their 'self-publishing' arms. Authors can be told that if their book does well under the 'self-publishing' imprint, they have a chance of being published by the traditional imprint. We have yet to hear of a transfer of this kind.

As an author, you should always check out hybrid publishers before working with them. Look up any candidates on the Preditors and Editors website;[16] search 'disputes with (name of company)' or 'problems with (name of company)' and see what comes up; and try to find at least one author who has worked with the company, if it hasn't been recommended to you by one. If they try to upsell you anything you didn't plan, want, need or budget for, look elsewhere.

Similarly, check the contract you are offered by a hybrid publisher with great care. At Rethink Press, our contracts are for the exclusive right to publish your work in print, e-book and audio book format in all territories for five years. We do not take control of your IP or restrict your ability to use your own material in other ways. If you wanted to end the contract early for almost any reason, we would release you from it, believing that an unhappy author or negative relationship is not working for either party. Some authors who have published with big 'self-publishing' companies have found themselves unable to get released from contracts they thought they had flexibility with.

Pros of hybrid publishing

Freedom, control and ownership: Your book is your own, and a reputable hybrid publisher will work with you to make your book exactly how you want

---

16   Preditors and Editors, http://pred-ed.com

and need it to be, in content, design and positioning. All professional hybrid publishers will tell you exactly what the cost of your publishing package is before starting work, and they will allow you to pay in reasonable instalments. This is much harder to do if you're managing your own team of freelancers/suppliers.

Professional production: The editor, designers and typesetter will be experienced in the business book genre, used to working with authors such as you and with each other. You will not have to source the professional contributors to your book, and with their input your book will have a thorough edit and proofread, and a professional look and feel.

Project management: As well as not having to search for the right professionals to create your book, the time-consuming and intensive task of managing them will be done by an experienced publisher, leaving you free to start marketing, working on your core business, and/or writing your next book. They will also manage your royalties and deal with queries and issues post-publication.

A real publisher: Although there is decreasing stigma about self-publishing, your book will have all the benefits of being produced and branded by a real publishing company. Like a traditional publisher, hybrid publishers have existing accounts with wholesalers, retailers, distribution databases and printers, so your book will have better distribution than a self-published book and your publisher will be able to access cheaper print rates than any individual author can. Some hybrid publishers of business books are well known and as aspirational as independent traditional publishers.

Quality: If you choose well, the end product will be high quality and professional. The edit, typeset, design and quality of your content should be top-notch – and a hybrid publisher will offer their professional advice and expertise while working to make your book what you need it to be for your brand and business.

High royalties: As you have taken a lot of the upfront risk of publishing your book, your hybrid publisher should be paying you higher royalties. At Rethink Press, we pay authors a royalty of 60% of net income on retail sales.

Easy access to stock: A good hybrid publisher will be transparent about costs should you wish to order author copies to sell direct. Because they're likely using a variety of POD and offset litho printers, it's possible to order very small or very large quantities at a decent price. In the case of Rethink Press, we pass on the print savings directly to our authors and keep pricing transparent. This means you only need to keep stock of a small quantity of books and you can top up stock at any time.

CASE STUDY – A NEW LEASE OF LIFE

Naasu G. Fofanah is a gender and global public policy expert. She is the Deputy Leader of the Unity Party Sierra Leone and Board Chairperson of the Sierra Leone Rugby Union. Naasu was Special Gender Adviser to the erstwhile President of Sierra Leone and former Vice Chair of the United Nations Economic Commission for Africa (UNECA) Bureau on Women and Development. She is an award-winning women's and girls' rights advocate. Despite her experience and qualifications, she had doubts that the book she wanted to write would ever find a publisher. She met Lucy at an event for women founders, explained the book she wanted to write and that she was actively seeking a female publisher. Although financially and emotionally low after major surgery, she was encouraged and given options and that made paid publishing an option. The support she received from the Rethink Press publishing team enabled Naasu to write and publish her book within seven months. She feels that her book *Leave It To Naasu* has given her a new lease of life.[17] She has been overwhelmed by the global response and the reception from Sierra Leoneans in particular. As well as buying the book, readers are also supporting Naasu's business. Reviews from the Sierra Leone diaspora across social media platforms have given Naasu and her book an increased authority and position in her country and internationally.

---

17   Naasu Genevieve Fofanah, *Leave it to Naasu: How to take charge and go for what you want* (Rethink Press, 2020)

Cons of hybrid publishing

Financial risk: There are hybrid publishers with packages to suit most pockets, but the author will always have to pay some upfront costs to get published. A good hybrid publisher will help an author to create a book that will easily return their investment through new and better clients and other ways of building their business.

Lack of marketing: Hybrid publishers may be able to offer PR and marketing support at a cost, but unless you invest in this – as with self-publishing – marketing and promotion is your job. You have to be the social marketer, PR agent and spokesperson for your book, and that means you'll need to spend time on getting a return on your investment – though not restricted to income from retail sales.

Distribution: Although your book may be listed with the wholesalers from whom physical bookstores order stock, it is less likely to find its way onto many physical bookstores' shelves unless it is your supportive local or specialist bookstore, or unless a customer orders your book through a bookshop.

Predators: There are 'self-publishing' companies who regularly take money from first-time authors and deliver poor services, publish low-quality books and badger their clients with up-selling offers for additional services, some of which – like marketing or PR packages – deliver no value. All authors should check out any hybrid publishing company before they sign contracts with or pay money to them.

As you will have realised, we are hybrid publishers at Rethink Press. Our business was set up to service successful expert entrepreneur authors like you because we strongly believe in this method of publishing.

Summary

Hybrid publishing is, we believe, the best route for a successful entrepreneur author, avoiding the barriers of traditional publishing and the pitfalls and lack of professionalism in DIY self-publishing.

Benefits include professional production, project management, a quality product, high royalties and access to author copies.

Conclusion

We wish you good luck with planning, writing and publishing the book that will transform your business.

In fact, you don't need luck – you just need to follow our process. But if you want to write your book with personal support from us or our Rethink Press coaching team, and in the company of a group of other successful entrepreneurs also writing their books, consider signing up to our Bookbuilder programme.

On the Bookbuilder programme, we work through positioning and planning your book on live group calls where each participant gets a private login to our unique MyBookPlan software and creates their book structure with the hands-on guidance of their own coach.

You will be a member of the private Bookbuilder Facebook group where we are constantly responsive to your questions and where you are part of an entrepreneur author community. You'll have access to coaching videos that take you step by step and in detail through the six steps of the WRITER process. And there are fortnightly group Zoom calls over the ninety-day programme, which will support you to get your transformative book planned and written through three drafts.

Go to www.bookbuilder.com and use the code 'BOOKBUILD' to get your discounted price for the next Bookbuilder programme.

Nothing sells you like a book. And no one builds your book like Rethink Press.

Acknowledgements

We would like to thank all the authors we have mentored and whose books we have published for allowing us to work with them on building their books. Every individual planning, writing and publishing journey brings us insight into how to do our job better, and your diverse business knowledge inspires us to make our business better.

We are proud of and indebted to the Rethink Press team, which comprises over forty international publishing professionals including coaches and writers, editors and designers, administrators and publishers. In particular, our Operations Manager Anke Ueberberg, Commissioning Editor Roger Waltham, Business Manager Matthew Flynn, Author Executives

Jennifer Scott and Alexander Tull, and Coaching Manager Siobhan Costello have contributed their creativity, skills and experience to building the business over the last few years.

Our production team on this book, from our Project Editor Helen Lanz, and copy editor Maya Berger, to our cover designer Jane Dixon-Smith and designer typesetter Lapiz have supported us throughout.

Our partners at Dent Global – Daniel Priestley, Glen Carlson, Mike Reid and Mike Clark – contribute their business acumen and support to Rethink Press, along with the indispensable Donna Bitten, Krizia Cureg, Rina Espiritu, Julie Pham and Carl Custodio.

And both our partners, Julie Gregory and Richard McCarraher, are vital members of Rethink Press and have supported us through getting *Bookbuilder* planned, written and published.

Thank you all!

The Authors

 **Joe Gregory**'s background is in advertising as a graphic designer, copywriter and marketer. He started his first business in 1997 specialising in online marketing, branding and promotion. In 2003, Joe co-wrote a book about his marketing approach and saw his business boom. The success of this self-published book led to the creation of Bookshaker – an independent publishing business which has helped hundreds of coaches, consultants, trainers and expert business owners get their work published to build their businesses. He is passionate about the power of books as a marketing tool and founded the hybrid publisher,

Rethink Press, with Lucy in 2011. His latest book, *Make Your Book Pay,* shows authors how to use their books strategically to grow their businesses.

Lucy McCarraher started her first publishing company while she was at university and has been involved in cutting-edge entrepreneurial ventures ever since. She is the Founder of Rethink Press, the Founder of the Business Book Awards and the Publish Mentor of Dent Global. Lucy is the author of thirteen books, including *A Book of One's Own – a manifesto for women to share their experience and make a difference, How To Write Your Book Without The Fuss and How To Write Fiction Without The Fuss.* She is an advocate for more women to write and publish their books. Lucy has worked in television and video on- and off-camera, and as a journalist, a business trainer and a work-life-balance consultant. She has a post-graduate diploma in teaching Creative Writing and Literacy, and she gives regular talks and workshops on writing and publishing.

If you've written your book and would like to discuss publishing with Rethink Press, get in touch to schedule a call at info@rethinkpress.com.

For more information, check our website at
www.rethinkpress.com.

And join us on social media at:

f www.facebook.com/rethinkpress

in www.linkedin.com/company/rethinkpress

⊙ @rethinkpress

y @rethinkpress

CPSIA information can be obtained
at www.ICGtesting.com
Printed in the USA
BVHW040439191220
596037BV00023B/919